country
CHRISTMAS

Country Christmas

Decorating the home for the festive season

Caroline Atkins

COLLINS & BROWN

First published in Great Britain in 2001
by Collins & Brown Limited
London House
Great Eastern Wharf
Parkgate Road
London SW11 4NQ

Distributed in the United States and Canada by Sterling Publishing Co.,
387 Park Avenue South
New York
NY 10016 USA

1 3 5 7 9 8 6 4 2

British Library Cataloguing-in-Publication Data:
A catalogue record for this book is available from the British Library.

ISBN 1 85585 912 2

Conceived, edited and designed by Collins & Brown Limited

Editor: Gillian Haslam
Copy Editor: Alison Wormleighton
Designer: Christine Wood

Reproduction by Classic Scan Pte Ltd, Singapore
Printed in the United States
This book was typeset using Bembo.

Contents

Introduction

The idea of Christmas in the country has an enduring quality that survives perennial attempts to give it a more urban, modern flavour. Even if the closest you usually get to it is the odd sheep on a snow-covered greetings card, it's hard to dispel the feeling that the countryside is where Christmas really happens. It represents the sense of peace and neighbourly companionship that we instinctively expect our celebrations to have, and it is where you'll find shepherds, stables, mistletoe and enough holly and ivy to garland the house in time for December 25th. But everyone has their own vision of the perfect country Christmas, and this book is about creating your own brand of country style to celebrate the festive season, mingling childhood memories with newer traditions, and combining homespun simplicity with richer delights.

The four main chapters provide four distinctive themes for your furnishings, decorations, gifts and greenery. Silver and gold conjure up classic elegance; hedgerow finds and garden greenery celebrate the

countryside's natural beauty; rich, dramatic colours and luxurious textures add traditional festivity; while bright wrappings and simple, streamlined settings are perfect for a more contemporary country Christmas. Each of these looks is recreated in the following pages, with beautiful rooms, welcoming hallways and a host of decorative details to inspire you. And for every theme there are suggestions for setting the table, making or wrapping presents, designing greetings cards to send to friends and family (and displaying those you receive) and creating delicious things to eat and drink.

The final chapter provides a host of ideas that can be used to dress up whichever look you choose. Projects for wreaths, candles, trees and stockings will help you create your own country Christmas, while angels, stars and berries will add a sprinkling of seasonal magic wherever they appear. Capturing all the spirit of the season, this book covers every part of the festivities – from hanging up the stockings to making your guests feel truly at home.

Holly & Ivy

Evergreen charm and hedgerow treasures

Hedgerow greenery, glowing berries, seedheads and fir cones all have a natural place indoors at this time of year, so this chapter celebrates the heart of the country, with all the natural beauty and colour it has to offer. Comfortable and welcoming, this is the classic country Christmas, a look epitomized by pine farmhouse tables piled with homemade treats, simple painted furniture festooned with greenery, and presents wrapped and decorated in natural materials. Although making the most of the informal, open-house approach, it somehow raises everyday pleasures to celebratory delights, so that the overall sense is one of indulgence and thanksgiving.

Dress your home with every shade of leaf green, trim it with berries in ruby red, golden yellow and milky white, and incorporate fruit, nuts, herb sprigs and cinnamon bundles to add the distinctive fragrance of the festive season. Bring the garden inside, making use of potting-shed materials such as hessian (burlap) and plain twine to tie up your presents, and gathering shrub prunings to weave into wreath bases. Find the flowers and seedheads you dried in the summer and autumn, and use them, along with any leftover evergreen sprays and cuttings, to design homemade cards and trim your gifts.

Plant your Christmas tree in a plain garden bucket or basket, and garland the hallway with plenty of mistletoe. Emphasize the natural theme by decorating the garden, too, adding to the overall sense of festivity.

Left: Rosehips from the hedgerow and logs from the garden. Bright berry decorations and a good supply of firewood are essentials for a classic country celebration.

Right: A country fireplace decorated with fir cones and hung with woollen stockings ready for Christmas morning. Wooden apple crates to hold larger gifts are labelled with the family's names.

Creating a welcome

Homecomings are an integral part of Christmas. After all the shopping, the preparations, the last-minute rush to complete office and school work, this is when the holiday really begins, as friends and families are reunited to celebrate the festival together. So extend the decorations to the outside of your house and make the entrance as welcoming as possible. Dress the doorway with greenery, light the path with lanterns – and then hope for a frost that will make everything sparkle just as it should.

Potted trees will create a miniature avenue leading to your front door. You can plant small Christmas trees especially for the season, or round up potted box or standard holly bushes already flourishing in other parts of the garden and move them into position. The greenery is really all you need to make an impact, but if you decorate the trees with tiny lights they will look even prettier and will light the way for your guests. Candle lanterns can be placed along the path between the trees, or hung across the gateway to create an illuminated arch.

Decorate your front door with the simplest wreath of all – a circle of gypsophila (baby's breath) whose tiny white flowers create a dusting of instant 'frost'. Use a floral-foam wreath tray as your base: soak it well, then pierce the foam with 5cm (2in) lengths of gypsophila, building them up around the ring until it is densely covered with frothy foliage and flowers. (You will need to water the wreath every two days to keep it fresh. To do this, lay it flat on a tray, fill the tray with water, then drain off the excess and hang in position again.)

Left: This festive doorway, flanked with fairy-lit fir trees and topped by a spray of blue spruce and traditional mistletoe, creates an instant sense of welcome.

Below left: An archway of hanging candle lanterns lights the steps to this flint farmhouse every Christmas. Additional candles sit among the little potted trees along the path.

Decorating with greenery

'Greenery' is so often used as a synonym for foliage that we tend to forget the variety of colour it can provide. Seasonal leaves come in a range of shades, from soft silvery grey to deep forest green, so make the most of these contrasts by combining different types of greenery to give your decorations extra richness. The beauty of natural foliage is that it never looks out of place: this is one good thing you can't have too much of, so you are free to use masses of it in complete confidence that the effect won't be over the top.

The main entrance area and living rooms are the first places your guests will see, so concentrate your efforts here. Swathe staircase banisters and newel posts, and even curtain poles, with lengths of twining foliage. Ivy is the easiest to use for this as it provides instant garlands that twist naturally and will cling in position wherever you place them. Add sprays of greenery behind pictures, clocks and mirrors. Extra boughs can be trimmed and arranged in jugs and vases around the house: make use of window-sills, table tops, even spare chairs.

Make swags and garlands to hang across fireplaces (keeping them well away from the flames), banisters and window-sills. Start with a length of heavy-gauge wire or strong jute cord. Using fine florist's wire, bind short lengths of evergreen such as cypress at the stems to form bunches, then attach these to the heavy wire or cord. They need to be close together to keep the swag or garland as thick as possible.

Greenery also provides its own natural 'accessories' which you can incorporate into your decorations, so look for fir cones and seedheads to wire into garlands and wreaths. For more variety in the colour scheme, combine them with dried

Left: A heavy double swag of pine cones and conifer decorates this candlelit fireplace. Additional sprigs of golden leaves on the mantelpiece catch the light and form a link between the natural foliage and the more opulent decorations on the shelf.

Right: Festive greenery in this hallway includes silvery green eucalyptus woven into a wreath, with the brighter shades of variegated ivy and clusters of golden hellebores decorating the staircase.

treasures preserved from the summer and autumn garden or gathered on country walks. Tightly furled roses, spiky teazels and thistles and copper beech leaves will all bring a sense of the hedgerow indoors and help keep your Christmas an authentically country affair.

Even a covering of lichen will add a soft, silvery bloom that looks very pretty among the decorations. A handful of lichen-clad twigs mixed with fir cones collected by the children makes a satisfying woodland display in a bowl on a window-sill. Include a few cinnamon sticks, too: the texture matches perfectly and you'll get a wonderful drift of Christmas scent every time you brush past them.

The paler shades of lichen and eucalyptus, pastel rose heads, and leaves that fade to a silvery grey when dried all give a slightly cooler, more minimal effect than the traditional lush winter evergreens. This allows you to create decorations that suit simpler furnishings and smaller rooms, where too much greenery might feel oppressive. Look for delicate ornaments such as dried allium heads and paper-thin, almost iridescent sprays of honesty to add to your arrangements.

Below: A garland of dried flowers and a wreath cut from paper leaves give an alternative twist to traditional Christmas greenery.

If you are running short of the real thing, you can supplement your decorations with a laurel or holly wreath made from leaves cut from stiff paper. The paper can be either painted pale green or left in its natural state – brown parcel paper, for example, will give an autumn-leaf effect. Cut out leaf shapes that are about 10–15cm (4–6in) long, and fold each in half lengthwise. Bend a length of thin galvanized wire into a circle about 40cm (16in) in diameter, then overwrap it loosely with a length of jeweller's wire. Now cut additional pieces of jeweller's wire – each about 6cm (2¼in) long – and tape one to the tip of each leaf as a stem. Use the wires to wind the leaves onto the wreath frame, working upwards around it on both sides until the circle is complete. As an interesting variation, you could cut the leaves from pages of text photocopied from a book onto stiff paper. You will need to copy the pages onto both sides. Look for text reflecting Christmas ideas (such as carol sheets or nativity descriptions from the Bible) or referring to trees and greenery, so that glimpses of the words turn the wreath into a sort of word-picture.

Below: Silvery green foliage provides a subtle background for splashes of bright berries in an old earthenware jug – the simplest of arrangements for a hallway or landing.

Below right: A bowl of fir cones makes a quick decoration for a window-sill. For fragrance, add some cinnamon sticks or sprinkle the cones with a few drops of scented oil.

The magic of mistletoe

The distinctive white berries and paired leaves of mistletoe appear like magic in apple orchards and on other trees at this time of year, growing in tumbling cascades without any evident roots. The source of numerous legends, this mysterious plant has been credited with extraordinary medical and supernatural powers – from fertility and aphrodisiac properties to an ability to cure cancer and epilepsy.

Although it remained long out of favour with the Christian church because of its pagan associations, mistletoe and the custom of kissing under it have gradually been incorporated into the Christmas tradition, so it is now an essential part of seasonal greenery. Hang a large bunch above doorways to create a festive welcome and work sprays of it into other arrangements. The pale green leaves combine well with foliage of different colours, and the gold-tinged berries provide a subtle contrast to the more usual bright red of holly and yew. Small sprigs can be tied with ribbon and hung on your Christmas tree, or planted in terracotta pots to create miniature 'trees' on window-sills.

If you are harvesting mistletoe straight from the orchard or hedgerow don't take too much. Cut only a little from each plant so that it will regenerate in time for next year. If you are buying it, look for bunches with strong, healthy-looking leaves and plenty of clustered berries.

Left: Mistletoe grows naturally in orchards, so it looks perfectly at home among the golden fruit decorations on this Christmas tree.

Right: Tie bunches of fresh mistletoe with ribbon or twine and hang them from beams and above doorways.

Winter harvest

Bowls of fruit and displays of ornamental vegetables and dried flowers help to add the abundance of a harvest festival to the winter colours of your Christmas celebrations. Combine them with church candles for a joyful, thanksgiving effect.

To create a table arrangement that makes the most of the natural ingredients available to you, cut a circle of floral foam to fit the centre of a plate. Soak it in water, then cut three or four holes in it to hold candles. Press the candles down into the holes until they feel secure. Add flowers and foliage, pushing the stems into the foam and building up the display gradually. Fresh or dried red roses will look wonderful combined with the crinkly deep purple and red-veined leaves of winter ornamental cabbages. Add dried hydrangeas too: their big heads fade into beautiful shades of golden red and silvery green in which leaves and petals seem to merge. When you are happy with the arrangement, place a few cinnamon sticks among the flowers and foliage so that their scent is released when the candles are lit.

For a simpler use of winter greenery, plain pillar candles can be decorated with an assortment of leaves and then placed among table displays or on bare window-sills. This is a similar technique to the dried-flower candles described on page 89. Melt paraffin wax in a double boiler, dip the leaves in it and position them on the candles in the design you want. Then dip the whole candle lightly in the melted wax, removing it carefully and leaving the wax to set into a protective layer over the leaves. For extra impact, stand the candles in front of a mirror or use them in lanterns so that the glass reflects the pattern of foliage.

Right: Russet-coloured apples are combined with fronds of evergreen and hanging gingerbread decorations to create a candlelit display in a Christmas window.

Below left: Leaves and ferns decorate these plain pillar candles, which make good presents as well as decoration for your home in winter.

Below: A simple but stunning arrangement of candles, roses, ornamental cabbages, dried hydrangeas and cinnamon sticks.

Classic wreaths

There is a completeness about the wreath shape that makes it a natural symbol of eternity. Enclosing and unifying, this simple circle has been used over the centuries as a mark of tribute, and at Christmas it represents a sense of unbroken peace, hopes and dreams.

Wreaths are not just for front doors: make them part of your table settings, use them as candle garlands, and hang them from ceilings and walls. To fix a wreath to a door or wall, attach a hanging loop of raffia or garden twine; or, for a more extravagant effect, hang the wreath from a length of festive ribbon. Alternatively, for an almost invisible means of support which doesn't involve making holes that will be in plain view all year round, use clear fishing line to hang the wreath from a nail fixed to the top of the door or picture rail. If you are making a ceiling decoration, attach four ribbons spaced equally around the circle so that the wreath can be hung horizontally from a beam or hook.

Natural greenery and hedgerow treasures are perfect ingredients to use for making wreaths. Weave twigs, stems and leafy fronds into circles and decorate them with berries, seedheads, herb bundles and fir cones. Start by looking for long, springy stems to use as your base: they need to be pliable enough to bend without splintering. Hazel and willow are ideal woods, but you need to bend them into shape while they are freshly cut – once they start to dry they will become more brittle and are liable to split. Avoid anything too prickly at this stage or you'll find the wreath difficult to work with when you try to add more decorations. If the wreath is going to consist of very dense greenery, you can make the base just from a length of strong wire twisted into a circle, safe in the knowledge that it won't show in the finished item. Easier to use, though, are the simple moss or twig circles sold by most florists; these will provide you with a basic country-style wreath ready to decorate with whatever ingredients you want.

Once you have the underlying shape, you can weave other elements into the wreath. Long-stemmed sprays are easy to work into position and anchor firmly; smaller pieces may have to be wired or glued into place. Keep a good supply of fine florist's wire handy as you work – it will prove invaluable for quick fixes. Vary the greenery you use by trying out alternatives to the traditional evergreens. Aromatic bay leaves create a fresh, herb-garden effect: gather leaf sprays into bundles and bind the stems tightly with garden twine

Left: This bright wreath combines a variety of country ingredients and creates a glorious splash of winter colour against the blue-painted door.

Above right: The subtle tones of pale bay leaves and white snowberries make a cool, elegant wreath to hang on a sea-green background.

or fine florist's wire, then tie the bundles onto the base, overlapping each other so that the stems are gradually hidden and the leaves fan out thickly. Decorate the wreath with unusual berries: pink-and-white snowberries make a delicate change from bright holly red, and the metallic-looking blue-black clusters of viburnum berries provide dramatic contrast among the greenery.

For something less formal and more rustic, incorporate fir cones and fruit, creating a celebration of country living in a single wreath. Start with a twig base and emphasize the woody effect by binding sections of textured bark into the circle, making the wreath look more substantial. You can also wind a length of hessian (burlap) or linen ribbon into it. Reminiscent of garden sacking, this will provide a useful base onto which ornaments can be pinned or stitched. Tie it into a bow at the bottom, for an added flourish. Your wreath is now strong enough to take shiny red apples, chunky fir cones, even dried artichoke heads among the mix. Go for lots of berries in different shades, such as hypericum, privet, cotoneaster and mistletoe, then add sprays of scented rosemary and bundles of cinnamon. As a final twist, echo the cinnamon sticks with little gold candles (not to be lit – just for decoration) tied with string and attached to the wreath in bunches.

Ivy, which is always pliable and easy to work with, will twist comfortably into a perfect wreath, and its pretty leaf shape makes an attractive addition to lighter, more delicate flower heads. Combine lengths of ivy with dried hydrangea heads and honesty sprays wound around a wire base and the result will be a beautifully natural Christmas wreath with the delicacy of a summer bouquet. For a cooler look – just as natural but with a frostier finish – try the thistle-like heads of silvery-blue eryngium.

Left: A simple circle of dried twigs interwoven with starburst heads of blue eryngium gives a frosty, wintry effect.

Right: The faded pinks and golds of dried hydrangea heads and honesty seedpods are offset by fresh ivy leaves in this front-door decoration.

The country table

The dining table is the heart of the home at Christmas. This is where everyone gathers to toast the season, give thanks, enjoy the company of family and friends – and finally get to sample all the food and drink that has been so painstakingly prepared over the last weeks. For a relaxed and inviting Christmas spread, set a refectory-style table that continues the idea of a winter harvest festival. Imagine that your dining room is a country barn, and fill it with greenery and candlelight for a celebration feast that everyone will remember.

Don't worry if your usual table isn't big enough for the number of guests – basic trestle tables (the sort used for wallpapering and as work benches) can be pressed into service as temporary substitutes. Once they are draped with traditional white tablecloths, the legs will be hidden and no one will be able to tell the difference.

Below left: For the simplest of place settings, top each plate with a pretty linen napkin and a piece of fruit.

Create one long table if you have enough room, or set them side by side, either as two separate tables or pushed together to form a wider rectangle.

Chairs don't need to be a matching set: when informality is the theme, furniture takes second place to the atmosphere and overall gaiety of the event. No one will mind what they are sitting on when the effect is so welcoming, and the variety of styles will reflect the harvest-supper feeling of simplicity and thanksgiving. Collect spares from around the house, adding seat cushions if necessary to make them comfortable. If you want to create a touch of decorative unity, dress the chair backs with fabric bows or sprays of greenery.

Mark each place setting with an extra gift, or tie a little gift bag or sack of gold chocolate coins to the chair back. Add plenty of fruit to the table, too, for colour

Below right: All set for the feast, a Christmas dining room decked with greenery and traditional Nativity figures. Gleaming candlesticks and gold-rimmed glasses add sparkle to the table.

and festivity and to provide a refreshing alternative to all the rich flavours and sweet sticky puddings that Christmas dinner invariably offers. Bowls piled high with clementines and grapes will act as instant decorations, and you can top each plate with a shiny red apple or pomegranate.

Add to the festive atmosphere at the table with plenty of candles. Reflected in the sparkling surfaces of glass and silverware, they will provide a rich glow that lifts the simplest setting to match the special occasion. Favourite china and glasses will look all the more beautiful in this soft, flickering light.

Greenery can play its part here as well. Ivy is a natural ornament for festive tables, as it will wind and trail beautifully among serving dishes and around candlesticks. Weave it into small circles to create instant napkin rings: this effect works beautifully on everything from plain white linen to cheerful checked gingham. You can tie a place name onto each ring, or trim it with berries for colour or cinnamon sticks for scent.

Holly is pricklier to deal with, but if you tie each napkin with raffia or coloured ribbon, it's easy to slip a berried sprig underneath for extra decoration. If you have a little more time, make holly balls to place on the table or display in glass dishes: stick individual leaves onto a ball of florist's foam until it is completely covered, then stud it with pretty glass- or pearl-headed dressmaker's pins to add sparkle.

Left: Laurel leaves stitched onto florist's wire create a glossy garland hung across this fireplace. The table is set with plenty of natural colour – fruit, berries and deep red roses – and the flickering fire adds to the glow of the candlelight.

Right: Woven twigs and ivy leaves make a simple napkin ring, with a painted wooden heart added to mark the guest's place at the table.

Chestnuts roasting on an open fire

Whether chopped into stuffing or cracked fresh from their shells, a supply of old-fashioned nuts is a must at Christmas. From glossy, polished pecans and hazelnuts to sweet-centred almonds and brazils, and those old frauds the walnuts, which look so tough but are soft and mellow inside, these wintry companions add flavour and texture to the oldest Christmas traditions. Sweet chestnuts are perhaps the most versatile of all. You can roast them on a tray in the oven or – more fun – over an open fire (first scoring a cross on each one so that the skin will peel off more easily when cooked). Add them to your stuffing, too, along with apples, apricots, parsnips or walnuts: choose your favourite combination for a delicious mixture that will bring out the flavour of the festive bird.

Serve a dish of fresh nuts at the end of the meal for your guests to enjoy along with the cheese and the fruit. The 'help yourself' principle is always convivial, extending the celebration by inviting everyone to join in the feast and linger at the table as long as they want. (Just provide as many nutcrackers as you can find: there are somehow never enough to go round, and people do tend to hang on to a set that is working well.) Try to choose a good range of cheeses so that there will be something for everyone – the classic cheeseboard includes hard, soft and blue varieties. However, you know your family's taste best, and it may be that a big wedge of well-matured farmhouse Cheddar is all you need to keep the party happy.

Right: Inside the spiky sweet-chestnut husks, the nuts themselves are hidden treasures just waiting to be used in your favourite Christmas recipes.

Below: Cheese and nuts will be in demand throughout the holiday. Add other treats such as dates, dried apricots and slices of sticky nougat.

Edible gifts

The original concept of bottling fruit in honey or sugar to preserve it gave way long ago to the making of jams and jellies as a treat in their own right, so jars of homemade preserves are always much appreciated as presents. Use crab apples, cranberries or bilberries in the mixture and your gift will also serve as a delicious accompaniment to the turkey on Christmas Day. Even seasonal staples such as mincemeat will make good presents, as well as being an essential ingredient in your Christmas cooking.

Making jam requires very high temperatures, so it's not really suitable for children to help with. If you want to keep younger members of the family occupied while you get on with the holiday preparations, let them loose on cakes and biscuits (cookies), which are fun for them to mix but do not involve hot pans of boiling liquid. One of the easiest recipes to try is Orange Jumbles – a traditional biscuit mixture incorporating oranges and almonds. Cream 115g (4oz, or ½ cup) caster (superfine) sugar with 85g (3oz, or 6 tablespoons) softened butter. Mix in

Below: A shelf of homemade preserves and fresh ingredients in a traditional country pantry. Jellies like these need to be kept still while they set, to prevent splitting; using smaller jars will also help.

115g (4 oz, or 1 cup) shredded almonds, 55g (2oz, or ½ cup) plain flour, the zest of two oranges and about 45ml (3 tablespoons) of the juice – the mixture should be soft but not sloppy. Drop teaspoonfuls of the mixture onto lined baking sheets and bake for 15–20 minutes, until thin and brittle, in an oven preheated to 170°C (325°F/gas mark 3).

Even more fun for children is to use a basic biscuit or shortbread recipe and then cut the rolled-out mixture into Christmas shapes before baking them. These make great gifts and can also be served as a snack along with the mince pies, or added to the table to accompany the pudding and brandy butter. Look for pastry cutters in the shape of stars, trees, reindeer or leaves – or let the children use their own artistic talents and create freehand designs. For extra sparkle, each one can be studded with little silver balls before baking. To turn them into presents, pack the finished biscuits into gift boxes or preserving jars, or wrap them in cellophane and tie with a length of ribbon, raffia or gold thread.

Below: A jar of cookies cut into cheerful Christmas shapes, including hand-decorated leaf designs.

Below right: Orange Jumbles are crunchy with almonds and easy to make. A few drops of cochineal can be added to vary the colour of the biscuits.

Cards from the garden

Evergreens and leaves collected from the garden can all be used to create homemade Christmas cards – from simple country-style images to more sophisticated designer effects. The secret is to pick strong leaf shapes so that they make their own visual statement. Maple, plane and sycamore leaves are all large enough to be used as a single image on a cardboard backing. The distinctive oak leaf shape is smaller but works well in a cluster or spray. Although holly is too prickly to use in this way, ivy – its fellow in the forest of the traditional carol – is perfect because the leaves will lie flat and are small enough to incorporate into a larger design.

Any cardboard or stiff paper can be used as your backing, but for the most artistic effect use sheets of textured watercolour paper torn into smaller pieces to create a deckle edging. The easiest way to do this is to paint a water line where you are going to tear the paper, let the water soak in, then pull the paper gently apart. Ensure the cards will fit a standard-sized envelope, otherwise you will end up having to make your own envelopes as well.

To build up the background panels for your leaves, add layers of foil or tissue paper, scraps of silk, muslin or other delicate fabrics, and fragments of elegant script. Apply squares of gold and silver metal leaf, or use sweet wrappers as an inexpensive alternative. Finally, glue the leaves in position, along with other decorations such as glass beads and wired ribbon.

Far left and near left: Cards made from watercolour paper are decorated with panels of hand-written script and ivy leaves on squares of gold and silver foil. Glass nuggets add an opulent finish.

Right: Fallen autumn leaves make simple designs on a background of plain stiff paper, and are also used here as templates for shapes cut from silver-birch bark. Holly, ivy or Christmas tree silhouettes cut out of bark would work equally well.

Calm & Bright

A contemporary country celebration

Christmas is about creating new traditions as well as celebrating the old ones, and this chapter is for anyone who wants a country Christmas with a contemporary twist. Combining a clean, fresh simplicity – reminiscent of the furnishings of Scandinavia and New England – with the irresistible sleigh-ride gaiety of the holiday season, it is full of bright, crisp ideas with zingy colours and streamlined style. This is a look for children to enjoy as much as adults: brimming over with sheer enjoyment, it's about having fun and taking things easy.

Making the most of natural decorations such as brightly coloured bark and freshly cut flower heads, it also incorporates newer elements like sparkling cellophane and sewing-box accessories. Sometimes it's just a question of using traditional ingredients in a new way – mixing tree ornaments with your card display or finishing your presents with an unexpected flourish of furnishing trimmings. Yet it also explores some of the most adaptable elements from modern decorating themes, bringing them into a country setting that softens their sophisticated edges while at the same time benefiting from their bolder colours. The winter shades of pink cyclamen and blue hyacinths, for example, work wonderfully when combined with pure snowy white to design plain boxy gift wrapping, beaded tree decorations and fresh table settings. Best of all, the ideas here all make the most of quick and easy effects, letting you turn on the festivities at the flick of a switch to create just the look you want for a 21st-century country Christmas.

Left: Gifts wrapped in crisp pink and white paper are tied with contrasting ribbons and trimmed with sprigs of herbs for an unexpected twist.

Right: Bright pinks and acid greens are mixed in among the traditional greenery for a Scandinavian-style celebration. The tree will be decorated late on Christmas Eve, to make a real impact in the morning.

Bright details

The secret of this slightly more contemporary look is its simplicity; there's nothing fussy or formal about its fresh colours and easy style. If you are worried about introducing different colours where you would normally keep to traditional red and holly green, just start slowly. Try out splashes of blue and yellow, lilac and lime green in small measures to gauge their effect and enjoy the contrast they provide among classic Christmas decorations.

The easiest feature to experiment with is the front-door wreath. This always makes an immediate impact and, because it is self-contained and doesn't need to match any other furnishings, it can incorporate new ideas and colours without disrupting an existing scheme. Try weaving different-coloured bark, such as stems of bright dogwood, into the circle, or trimming it with cheerful ribbons.

Table decorations can be used to add small elements of unexpected colour to a more traditional arrangement. With a plain background of crisp white table linen, you can introduce all sorts of new shades with flowers and place settings. Again, keep the whole effect as simple as possible. Put tiny pots of fresh flowers or dried roses as a gift at each place, and tie white napkins with a mixture of bright ribbons. For an after-dinner treat, include handfuls of rainbow-coloured sweets (candy) or sugared almonds among the dishes of gold and silver dragées.

Right: The glorious rainbow shades of dogwood bark weave together beautifully to make a wreath glowing with winter colour in contrast with silvery pussy willow.

Below left: Some flowers actually gain in intensity of colour when they are dried. A miniature bucket of bright dried roses looks breathtakingly simple when combined with hand-painted cards, crisp white table linen and pure white candles.

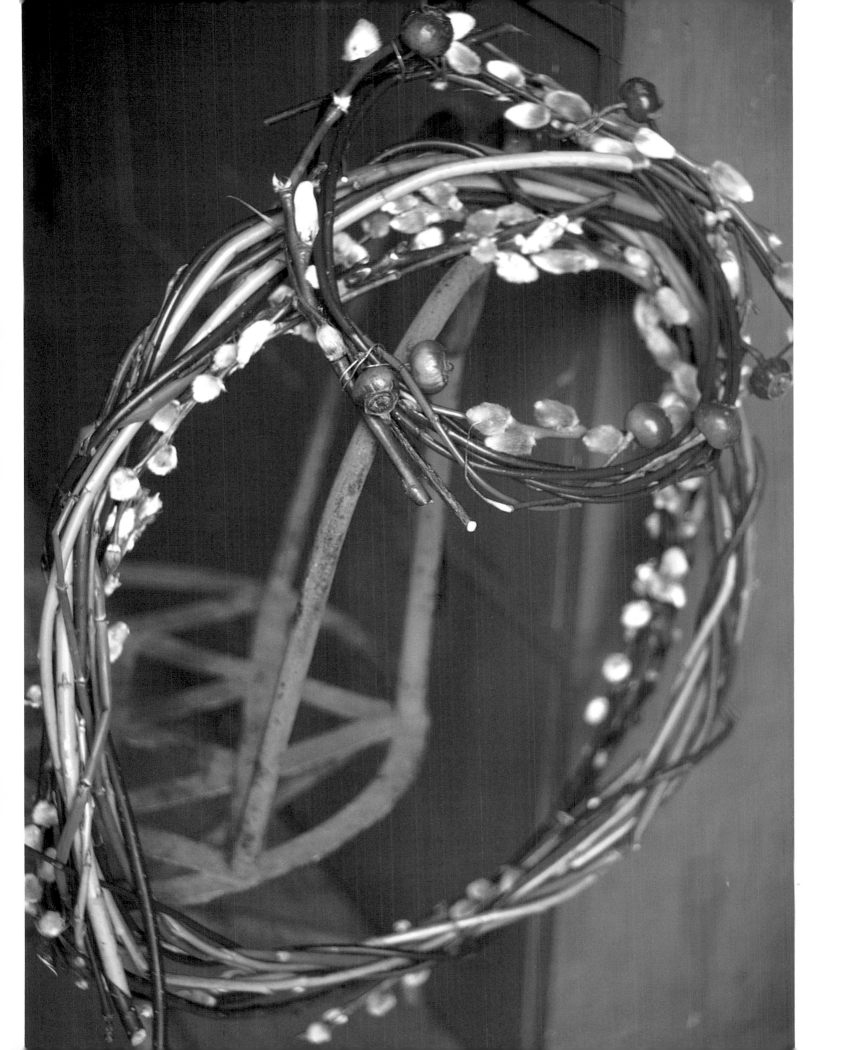

Once you have mastered the knack of thinking laterally like this, it becomes easier to push out the boundaries of classic Christmas decorations and look in unusual places for ideas. Haberdashery (notions) departments, for instance, are a mine of inspiration, because those rolls of braid and coils of ribbon hold all the tradition you want from a country Christmas – and yet also contain dozens of colours you won't have thought of incorporating in the decorations at this time of year. Use braid, ribbon and bright silk thread to wrap presents, hang tree decorations and tie gift tags onto parcels.

Fabric scraps can be pressed into service too. Lengths of soft felt in primary colours are ideal for cutting with pinking shears into neat gift tags. You can also use felt for making personalized stockings: just cut simple sock shapes and stitch or glue them together around the edges in pairs, leaving the tops open ready to be filled. It's not surprising that the effect is reminiscent of children's toys and school sewing kits – the bright colours and simple shapes lend themselves to children's decorations. (They make it easy for you to involve the children, too: pinking shears are safe for them to use, and fabrics can be glued rather than stitched if you want to avoid sharp needles.)

If you want a more sophisticated finish, look for elegant tassels to trim your trees, presents and furniture. A flourish of multicoloured cord will look stunning hung from each chair back around the festive table, attached to door handles, decorating the largest presents or dressing up the tub that holds your Christmas tree. You can also use tassels to display your cards: just fix one end of the cord to the picture rail, pin the cards down its length and let the weight of the tassel at the bottom hold the arrangement in place.

Of course, one of the most natural styles to create with clean lines and plain colours is the Shaker look, so if you want a traditional New England Christmas, go for checked wrapping paper, gingham ribbons hung on the wall to display your cards, painted wooden tree decorations and gingham fabric stockings. Gift labels and place cards can be cut from thick foil and 'engraved' to look like pressed tin. Just write on them with a ballpoint pen – the ink won't take on such a smooth surface, but the point will leave a clear impression. Or use copper plant labels for the same effect.

Left: Raid your sewing box, rediscover your local haberdashery (notions) department and rummage in remnant sales for scraps of bright fabrics to make labels and Christmas stockings. Use cord and tassels to dress up furniture, and embroidery floss to thread through gift tags.

Right: Painted wooden hearts threaded together with plain twine create Shaker-style decorations for the tree, doors or chair backs. Use muted colours for a gentle effect or zingy brights to keep the look crisp and modern.

Winter flowers

Amid all the evergreen foliage that traditionally fills our homes at this time of year, the clear colours and fresh scent of cut or potted blooms make a refreshing contrast. Use them to brighten up bathrooms and guest bedrooms (where prickly holly and trailing ivy aren't the most practical form of decoration). Include several vases on your dining table, to offset the greenery. Flowers make wonderful gifts, too – ideal to take as a present for your host, and appreciated every bit as much as the ubiquitous chocolates and bottles of sherry. The simplest effects are the best, so go for a mass of one colour rather than an elaborate mix. Bundles of white narcissi, bowls of pink cyclamen and proud hyacinth heads in shades of pink, blue, white or cream provide an irresistible splash of spring-like colour in the depths of winter.

The promise of pale green hyacinth shoots, holding just a hint of the colour that's going to burst from them, is almost as delicious as the blooms themselves, so enjoy every moment of anticipation. If you're giving them as a present, choose hyacinths that are not quite flowering, so that the best is still to come. To grow your own, plant the bulbs around three months before Christmas to have them

Below left: Massed heads of white narcissi exude a wonderfully heady fragrance. To keep a display like this fresh, tie 15 or 20 stems together, push them into well-soaked floral foam and cover with moss.

ready by December 25th, keeping them in a cool, dark place for eight to ten weeks after potting and then bringing them into the light. (Don't force them with too much heat: this will just create long stems and scanty flowers.) The more intense their colour, the stronger the scent, so choose deep blues and pinks for maximum effect or classic white if you prefer something less overpowering.

If you haven't time to grow narcissi from bulbs, you can create a densely 'planted' effect in just a couple of minutes by taking a bunch of cut flowers, tying them neatly at the top and bottom and pushing the stems into a bowl of well-soaked floral foam. Cover the foam with moss and keep it well watered – the narcissi will look as though they grew here naturally.

Other cut flowers that add bright colour at Christmas include anemones (try mixing the dramatic purple shades with blue hyacinths for a really vivid effect) and chrysanthemums. To keep the look cool and modern, avoid the traditional autumnal reds and golds and raid your local florist for the amazing green-petalled chrysanthemums that many designers use in contemporary table settings.

Below right: Bright hyacinths make glorious presents at this time of year as well as providing scent and decoration for your home. Look for unusual containers such as little aluminium buckets or painted pots, and decorate them with festive ribbons.

Homemade presents

One way to bring more colour into Christmas is to make your own presents, using fresh paint shades and remnants of bright fabric and paper. Your one-off designs will be appreciated all the more for their individuality. Many of these ideas are simple enough to double as tree decorations, but with a little more effort they can be turned into covetable gifts.

Paint works like magic to transform everyday accessories. Wooden mirror and photograph frames, which are ideal presents, can be brightened up with a quick coat of colour. If you are feeling more creative, add extra decoration such as layers of silver or gold leaf (see page 67 for how to apply metal leaf). Terracotta flowerpots can be turned into cheerful containers for sweets and chocolates or, appropriately, flower bulbs and packets of seeds. Plain white china is a perfect background for hand-painted patterns: take inspiration from the success of the pottery cafés now springing up everywhere and decorate mugs, milk jugs and egg cups with individual designs to suit the recipient.

Even household basics such as kitchen trays – available as MDF (medium-density fibreboard) 'blanks' ready for you to paint – and wooden coat hangers

Below: Paints in crisp, fresh shades can be used to decorate homemade gifts. Give trinket boxes, china and photo frames a bright finish for an individual touch, and design your own Christmas cards on sheets of watercolour paper.

become attractive presents with a coat of colour. Plain wooden boxes, perfect for storing jewellery and trinkets or, in their larger sizes, bedroom and bathroom accessories, can often be bought in MDF sets. Oval Shaker-style boxes can be painted, too, but the traditional ones fashioned from curved lengths of cherrywood are best left natural. Decorated or plain, Shaker boxes become instant packaging as well as gifts in their own right. Old cigar boxes will also acquire a new lease of life if given the paint treatment.

The trick is to think before you throw anything out. Remnants and leftovers are key ingredients for the creative gift-maker, so hoarders will have a natural advantage when it comes to looking for inspiration and materials. Leftover paint and unused tester pots are classic examples. Find somewhere safe and accessible to store them as there will always be a use for good colours, and small quantities are often all you need.

Paint small chips of wood in bright colours to make one-off gift tags (just drill a hole in one corner and thread through a length of twine or ribbon). Or design individual labels and messages suitable for specific recipients: nameplates for children's bedrooms and signs directing visitors to 'the garden' or 'the potting shed' or other well-used places.

Fabric scraps are even more versatile. Save offcuts from dressmaking and furnishing materials and use them to make lavender bags. Cut a rectangle of fabric twice the size of the bag you want, fold it in half (right sides together), then stitch up the two sides, leaving the top open. Turn the bag right side out, and trim the top edges using pinking shears to stop them from fraying. Fill with dried lavender and tie a ribbon or cord around the neck to close the bag. An even easier variation is to fold lengths of wide ribbon, instead of fabric, in half crosswise, and stitch the two opposite sides to create instant bags. Thread a few beads onto the cord or ribbon, knotting it to hold them in place, and your handiwork will look every bit as stylish as the designer gifts on sale in the smartest stores.

Instead of lavender, you could buy a quantity of loose pot-pourri and use this to fill several of these fabric bags. Or, for a different type of scented present, make larger bags in the same way, and fill them with little soaps or bath cubes. In fact, bags like these can be used to hold all sorts of gifts. For children, brightly coloured pouches of sweets (candy), marbles or tiny toys are ideal.

You could give the bag a more professional finish by leaving an extra length at the top so that instead of a drawstring fastening, you create a flap that will fold over like an envelope and can be sealed neatly with a decorative button. If you adapt this idea in a larger format, you could fill the bag with herbs to make a little cushion.

Special presents merit special treatment, so why not develop the ideas suggested here to create individual gift bags from bright silk or velvet that the recipient will want to keep along with the contents? A piece of jewellery, a rolled silk scarf or a beautifully designed pen would all benefit from this treatment.

Below: Lengths of bright silk ribbon with a decorative edge have been folded in half and stitched into little herb pouches. Fill them with lavender, rose petals or other favourite scents and tie with fine ribbon to make tree presents or stocking fillers.

Open gifts

Make the most of interesting containers to create readymade gift packaging and brighten up your festive table. Even the most functional items – pottery mugs, little aluminium flower buckets or terracotta pots – can be made to look decorative and appealing. Filled with sweets (candy), fruit, nuts or other edible treats, they can be given as presents or put on the table as part of the celebrations. You can let guests help themselves, or set a small individual pot next to each place setting.

The beauty of this idea is that it's so quick and easy. There is no actual wrapping involved – just the combination of a suitable container and intriguing contents. And as the contents aren't hidden away, the gift becomes an open invitation, encouraging people to dip in.

You could mix up unwrapped chocolates from a conventional box and let people pick them as a lucky dip, without the 'key' that tells people which flavours they are – it all adds to the fun. Wrapped sweets or chocolates are particularly colourful, while gold chocolate coins and foil-covered peppermint creams are old favourites that guests of all ages will enjoy. Children will love lollipops or toffee apples wrapped in bright cellophane and presented stick side up, ready for them to take their pick.

Left: Toffee apples wrapped in jewel-coloured cellophane provide an irresistible treat after country walks and carol singing. Present them in a shallow dish or pack them into gift boxes – shoeboxes covered in festive paper are ideal.

Right: Old-fashioned jelly moulds and tins make unusual containers for home-baked goodies. Line them with a layer of clear Cellophane and tie with a length of ribbon.

Creative gift wrapping

The simpler the wrapping, the more enticing the contents of the gift become. Like a mask, the wrapping gives no hint of what's underneath, yet makes the recipient all the more impatient to find out. Taking a leaf out of the contemporary book means keeping the trimmings to a minimum and opting for plain colours, neat boxes, brown parcel paper and string. Some gifts need barely be wrapped at all: instead, just let the modern alternative – smart paper carrier bags – create a wonderfully new, fresh-from-the-shop feel.

Coloured papers are available all year round, not just at Christmas. Sheets of tissue and crêpe paper are sold in multiple packs in craft shops as well as in stationers'. For value for money, choose crêpe: it goes much further than tissue as you only need a single layer to disguise what you are wrapping. Pick a bright colour, then find a contrasting cord, braid or ribbon to tie it up for a classic parcel effect. Of course, with all the various types of cellophane tape available today, this additional binding is no longer strictly necessary, but it provides an extra dash of intrigue – another layer to be undone.

To make the parcel ultra-smart, add a blob of sealing wax and emboss it with a stamped design. Sealing wax kits are available complete with initial stamps so that

Left: Update traditional Christmas colours and include wrapping in vibrant shades such as shocking pink to clash with classic red for a jazzy, flamboyant effect. Stack your presents under a tree trimmed with zingy pinks and greens and contemporary white paper stars.

Right: Plain crêpe paper in bright colours makes stunningly simple parcels. Tie with ribbon and finish with blobs of red sealing wax.

53

you can add a personal touch with the first letter of your name. Otherwise, use melted candle wax to create the same effect, impressing it while it is still soft with a relief-patterned metal button.

As an alternative to the criss-cross style of parcel ties, you can encircle wrapped presents with bands of ribbon and braid, layering different fabrics, widths and colours. This effect gives the simplest paper a really luxurious finish, and you can just slip a card or gift tag under the band. Or, for a touch of romance, glue tiny satin or velvet flowers, such as the little ribbon rosebuds you find in haberdashery (notions) departments, onto the paper – either sprinkled all over or in a cluster beside your label.

Some presents benefit from being boxed or bagged rather than wrapped. Anything with a shape that has awkward corners or is hard to disguise (such as a bottle of wine or champagne) will look clumsy or downright obvious, however many layers of paper you wrap it in, so take a tip from the merchandisers and choose packaging that makes a virtue of necessity. By making the most of its best features, you can turn the most mundane item into a must-have delight. Think of the elegant boxes used to package special stationery and luxury lingerie, and use the same principle to create the 'presentation' factor. Save useful boxes: practical box files in pretty colours are ideal for wrapping accessories like scarves and lingerie and will turn even towels or pillowcases into desirable gifts. Just add ribbons – to decorate the items themselves as well as tied around the boxes. Presents that come in several parts, such as sets of glasses or bathroom treats, can be individually wrapped in tissue paper and loosely packed in little paper carrier bags. Decorate the bags with colourful ribbon and bright Christmas images, and use extra tissue to fill the open tops.

Below far left: Pretty coloured box files are perfect packaging for special gifts. Wrap the contents in tissue paper and decorate the box with lengths of ribbon and flowers.

Below left: Use ribbon and braid in different widths and colours to add a smart banded finish to plain wrapping.

Right: Small carrier bags (the sort used by sandwich shops) make ideal gift bags when trimmed with ribbons and filled with colourful tissue paper.

Above: A 'curtain' of cards and glass baubles hung on fine wires creates a sparkling effect across the corner of a room. You can create a colour scheme with carefully chosen shades, or go for a more random, celebratory mix.

Left: A collection of colourful homemade cards created from layers of different-textured papers makes a strong impact when hung from plain tapes and finished with glowing crystal droplets.

Displaying cards

The cards we receive at Christmas are a celebration of friendship, and putting them on show creates a sort of universal greeting as well as adding festive colour to our homes. But there are never enough mantelpieces, shelves, table tops and window-sills to hold them all, so additional display arrangements are always useful. The secret is to make the most of hanging space by suspending cards from walls and ceilings. This works best if you combine them with other decorations to highlight their colours and accentuate their design.

The easiest trick is to pin the cards onto lengths of ribbon fixed to a picture rail. Choose a ribbon colour that picks out the colours of the images, and try to weight the end so that it won't be disturbed by draughts. A heavy tassel is ideal for this (see page 45) or, for a cooler, more elegant finish, try the jewel-coloured crystal droplets sold in antique lighting shops as replacement chandelier fittings. These add a designer twist and a wonderful glow reminiscent of tree baubles. You don't need to cover a complete wall like this: it's such a special effect that it will work just as well for a display of a few favourite cards.

For an even more dramatic effect, create a curtain or swag of hanging cards, suspended so that the individual items can turn freely, almost like a decorative mobile. You need a high ceiling for this so that the display stays clear of people's heads. Otherwise, hang it across a corner of the room where it won't be in the way. Fix an evergreen branch to the ceiling to support the decoration. Choose a selection of cards whose colours work well together, then make a hole in the corner of each and thread a length of fine wire through it, twisting the end back on itself to hold the card firm. Now fix the other end of the wire to the support branch. Vary the lengths of the wires so that the cards hang at different heights and, to complete the effect, add gleaming glass Christmas tree balls – some hung on their own wires, others threaded onto the wires that hold the cards.

It's always a delight to receive homemade greetings, and if you'd like to send your own this year, they need not be time-consuming to make. The trick is to keep your designs simple and let colour and texture do the work. Stylized shapes in strong colours will always make an impact, and layering contrasting papers creates an informal effect that doesn't require straight lines or perfectly trimmed edges. Use stiff cardboard or heavy cartridge paper (poster board) as your base, then add a mixture of decorative and lightweight papers such as tissue and crêpe paper and pressed-flower gift wrap. For sparkle, include silver and gold foil in your design, too. Motifs can be cut out of coloured paper or printed with a stamp or potato-cut shape.

Fire & Frost

The classic elegance of silver and gold

Silver and gold are the most versatile of all the Christmas colours, taking in elegant shades of white and cream, stone and grey, as well as the traditional festive metallics. Rich in both appearance and symbolism, they will let you experiment with a range of decorating schemes, from simple and elegant to sparkling and opulent. Don't worry if your home isn't well stocked with supplies of the real thing: there are a host of ways to create your own silver and gold once you know how. Use the cooler tones to conjure up the magic of snow and frost; or add a sense of seasonal warmth with golden candlelight and clove-studded oranges. Incorporate fabrics that gleam and shimmer; set the table with gold-rimmed glasses and add mother-of-pearl cutlery to catch the light.

This chapter brings together sophisticated metallic and lustre finishes with the natural country colours of faded greenery, glowing marmalades and farmhouse pine furniture. It shows you how to transform accessories with a layer of gold or silver leaf, design glamorous packaging to dress up your presents, and gild leaves and berries to make your Christmas evergreens more luxurious. There are recipes for sugar frosting to decorate seasonal delights and golden brandy punch to warm your guests, as well as suggestions for using dried fruit to create aromatic garlands and tree ornaments. Gold and silver make a timeless combination that looks just as effective with contemporary furnishings as it does in a more traditional setting.

Left: Traditional gingerbread becomes even more of a treat when finished with a layer of edible gold leaf. A single square (from art shops or specialist cake-decorating suppliers) laid in a diamond pattern creates the impression of a star.

Right: Gold and silver sparkle together in this candlelit window, where shortbread biscuits have been turned into hanging decorations with glowing fruit centres.

All that glisters

Gold and silver conjure up instant festivity and, because they create a readymade colour scheme, are also among the easiest shades to use for decorating your home at Christmas. The smallest amounts will add lustre and shimmer, so if you stick to this classic palette you will create the most elegant of effects with the minimum of effort. If you are faint-hearted about using such opulent colours, start by trying them out in small quantities: just hanging a silver wreath on a door or a gold tassel from the door handle will show you how effective a simple touch can be.

These are shades that combine wonderfully with rich blues, reds and greens for a dramatic, opulent effect – ideal for creating a celebratory atmosphere in a dining room, complete with flickering candlelight and a blazing log fire. They will also blend gently with pastel shades of blue, coral and aqua for an elegant look reminiscent of faded Regency splendour or the cool tranquillity of Gustavian furnishings. And for the simplest, most timeless look of all, use gold and silver against a background of pure cream or white, so that the metallic tones are seen as colours in their own right, adding depth and definition to the room and letting you experiment with a glorious range of shades, from the palest silver to deep burnished bronze.

Candlelight will create even more sparkle by glowing in all those reflective surfaces, and you can enrich this effect with mirrors. If you have a good-sized mirror, above a mantelpiece perhaps, make the most of it by dressing it with gilded decorations where they will be reflected for double the impact. Arrange candles along the mantelpiece in gold containers – anything from traditional candlesticks to gold-painted flowerpots. For more lustre, decorate the candles themselves with

Left: Bay leaves bound onto florist's wire create a simple circlet decorating this door handle. The overlapping leaves form a miniature wreath which can then be sprayed with gold paint.

Right: This mantelpiece with its elegant overmantel mirror has been dressed with a luxurious garland of gilded leaves, fir cones, seedheads and ribbons. Candles set in little flowerpots are decorated around their bases with gold-painted nuts and shells.

silver or gold leaf. Add sprays of gilded leaves between them, and any gold or gilt-patterned balls left over from the tree, then swag the whole shelf with a gilded garland woven from greenery and seedheads.

Some of the best gold and silver decorations aren't specifically designed for Christmas, but are versatile enough to make your home glow all year round. Metallic paints and wallpapers and lustrous fabrics can be combined with gold and silver leaf as well as actual metal surfaces to cast a shimmer over the whole room. Look for fabrics that have their own sheen, and for the Christmas period resurrect old cushion covers, curtains and throws that will add to the magical effect. Brocades and woven silks, shiny satin ribbons, crisp, sparkling organza, and velvet with its rich pile, catching the light when it is brushed in the right direction, will all reflect the light beautifully.

The secret is to aim for a pale gleam rather than a gaudy glitter. Transform old chairs with a layer of silver paint, stippled with a dry brush so that the finish appears as a light dusting of silver rather than anything too bright. This treatment will make even shabby garden furniture look good enough to bring indoors. Rub gilt cream (from craft and art shops) onto wooden accessories such as mirror and picture frames, distressing the finish slightly to keep it mellow. Include elements of unpolished pewter, too: this will introduce a more muted, less opulent note, emphasizing the sense of beautiful materials used for a functional purpose rather than purely for decoration. Then, to lift the setting out of the everyday and give it a touch of extra luxury for the season of celebration, mix your metallics with the iridescent surfaces of mother-of-pearl and old-fashioned lustreware. Dress the dining table with cutlery and china in these delicate finishes, and add classic white porcelain decorated with gold and silver patterning.

Left: The pale gleam of classic silver candlesticks and elegant gold-patterned china blends beautifully with the pastel shades of late roses on this white-painted mantelpiece.

Below right: Rich gold brocade and soft silver velvet create luxurious cushions against a plain white background. Look for metallic braids and trimmings to decorate your furnishings with extra festive sparkle.

Gilded leaves

The real magic of gold and silver is the way they instantly transform everything they touch. Furniture, fabrics, flower heads, nuts and greenery can all be given the metallic treatment to turn your home into a temporary treasure house for the Christmas season. The quickest method of all is to use gold and silver sprays. These are available from art shops and are easy to work with (although you need to keep the room well ventilated during the process). Apply the spray in thin coats so that you can vary the thickness of the gilding and control the finished effect – from a pale dusting to a deep, rich gold. This will work on fabric and trimmings as well as on solid surfaces.

For a more dramatic, professional look, use sheets of real gold or silver leaf, or try Dutch metal, which is applied in much the same way as traditional metal leaf but is cheaper to buy. All you need to do is paint on a layer of artist's size to act as an adhesive, then, once the size is transparent and tacky, press on the sheets of Dutch metal, smoothing them down with your fingers until the surface you are decorating is completely covered.

If you prefer working with a paintbrush, try bronze powders, which come in a range of different shades and create a dusty, antique feel. You need to wear a mask while applying them. The powders are brushed on over a layer of size, gently burnished to give a more polished effect and then varnished to secure the finish. Gold wax is another alternative; this is applied with a soft brush and then burnished with a soft cloth.

Experiment with the different techniques to see which you feel most comfortable with, then start creating decorations of your own. Greenery makes an excellent base, because the distinctive leaf shapes and the relief patterns traced by their veining are such strong design elements, and gilding them highlights these features very effectively. A simple arrangement of leaves such as laurel, bay and holly will look stunning if sprayed with gold and displayed in a sparkling glass vase. These are perfect leaves to use as they are strong and glossy and will hold their shape well under the gilding.

More delicate leaves can be worked into a design that gives them strength and structure – as part of a larger garland, for instance. Or they could be combined with other leaves to decorate a cardboard-backed wreath. Wreaths like this are simple to make. Select your leaves (oak, beech, lime and sweet chestnut will all work well as they provide a variety of shapes and are similar to each other in weight) and spray them with gold and silver. Cut a thin ring out of stiff cardboard,

Left: A bunch of gilded laurel and bay leaves creates a simple decoration for a table or mantelpiece. The leaves have been sprayed quite lightly in places so that the green shows through for a more natural effect.

and mount the leaves on it, overlapping them slightly so that by the time you have completed the ring the cardboard isn't visible. Alternate the shapes and the metallic colours so the finished wreath has plenty of interest and depth of tone. For the most dramatic effect, hang it against a deep background or on a dark-painted door so that the shimmering surface of the leaves creates a bright contrast.

These elegant colours also combine well with natural, ungilded greenery, so mix them in your decorations. Mistletoe works particularly well, as its berries have a pale gold tinge that is beautifully highlighted by the accents of metallic gold (see page 80), and snowberries will gleam like pearls when set among gilded leaves. A mixture of gilded and natural ivy lengths will look equally effective. For a touch of real decadence, gild a plain wooden curtain pole, along with its rings and finials, and then wind ivy strands around it so that the whole window becomes a gloriously baroque affair.

Left: A wreath of mixed leaves has been sprayed in different shades of gold and silver and trimmed with a raffia ribbon to make a bright decoration for this deep-blue panelled wall.

Right: A spray of gilded walnuts and leaves is pegged together with a bunch of berried mistletoe to make the easiest of decorations, suitable for use either indoors or out.

An elegant setting

Dress your dining room in gold and silver for the most elegant table setting of all. Adjust the levels of gold and silver according to how rich you want the final effect to be. If you are worried that the effect will be too opulent, keep things subtle by sticking to plain white or cream china on white damask linen and adding touches of gold and silver in the accessories. Gleaming silver cutlery, napkin rings and candlesticks will be enough to create a celebratory sparkle, with the pale gold of candlelight and champagne adding a warm glow.

The more gold you introduce, the more sumptuous the look will be. Setting the table with gold-rimmed china and glasses will add to the festivity of the occasion, and gold party trimmings such as crackers and paper napkins will provide extra colour quickly if your china cabinet is running low on opulent tableware. Alternatively, look for proper napkins in glittering organza, or buy a length of gold fabric and stitch your own. Just for fun, you can tie the cutlery into little individual bundles with metallic ribbon – or, for a neat, more contemporary finish to the table, turn them into boxed sets by buying flat gold boxes (from stationery shops), lining the boxes with tissue paper and binding them with ribbon or raffia so that each guest has an extra 'gift' to open before the meal.

Silver trimmings will also add sparkle but are slightly subtler, providing a glow of moonshine and starlight and letting you combine traditional decorations with more modern elements. Decorating your dining room with silvered greenery

Left: A gilded nest of sugared almonds trimmed with glittering ribbon sits alongside a cluster of gold-painted acorns and a jug of rich yellow candles.

Right: The perfect balance of gold and silver decorations gives this dining room a natural elegance. Classic cream tableware completes the setting.

rather than gold, for instance, will maintain a cool elegance, evoking a sense of winter frost that echoes the sugar icing on your Christmas cake.

Make the most of natural gold tones, too, using traditional country elements to create a less formal ambience in which to enjoy the gathering of friends and family for meals throughout the holiday. Even if you want a more elaborate spread for Christmas dinner itself, you can incorporate simpler decorations into a relaxed setting that is perfect for the pleasures of Christmas Eve supper, in anticipation of the celebrations ahead, or for Boxing Day brunch, when the excesses are over and you can recover in quieter mood. The mellow tones of honey-coloured wood and harvest-gold dried greenery will all add to the welcoming, comfortable feel and conjure up the atmosphere of an old-fashioned country kitchen. Don't cover up your old pine table: let the natural colour provide a background for the feast. Make wreaths from woven grasses and trim your presents and decorations with gold-coloured twine. Add yellow beeswax candles and natural-coloured serving baskets.

The food itself provides its own riches – from buttery yellow shortbread to crunchy golden cookies and oatcakes, dishes of polished chestnuts (see page 32) and fruit stands piled with glowing oranges, kumquats and clementines. Use nests of woven twigs – either in their natural colour or highlighted with a coat of metallic spray – as alternative containers for treats and sweets. Chocolate coins, foil-wrapped fudge or toffees and sparkling gold and silver sugared almonds will look all the more tempting presented in this way.

For extra festivity, decorate the walls and ceiling of your dining room with wreaths of gold and silver greenery. As well as gilding leaves with metal leaf or paint, look for natural materials that provide their own winter colour. Sprays of silver pussy willow are soft and velvety, while hedgerow finds such as old-man's-beard (wild clematis) can easily be twisted into loosely woven circles for a country-style garland.

By taking your cue from the muted colours of these natural decorations, you can also work subtler shades into the colour scheme of your furnishings and table settings, toning bright gold down into taupe, stone and coffee, for instance. This works particularly well in contemporary-style homes, where you want to create an effect of subdued elegance rather than traditional Christmas glitter. The tones of pale gold and coffee are surprisingly close. Combined with cream and white, they make a delicious mix that is every bit as rich as the metallic surfaces but much warmer and more relaxed – just the setting you need, in fact, to enjoy your best Christmas ever.

Left: A ceiling-hung wreath decorated with gilded oak leaves and ornamental birds provides the centrepiece for a celebratory table setting, while a loosely woven circle of dried grasses creates a decoration for the wall. The rich gold of the traditional farmhouse furniture gives the room its own natural glow.

Frosted fruits

Crisp, cold, frosty weather is what everyone associates with Christmas. But you can't count on it so conjure up your own sparkle with sugar-frosted fruits. Position them in windows where they will catch the light, display them in cut glass or arrange them on candlelit tables for a gloriously baroque, opulent setting.

Almost any smooth-skinned fruit will respond well to this treatment, so try out different pieces for varying effects. Look for a contrast between the colour and the frosting: glowing golds and oranges and deep plum colours look especially dramatic. Wipe the fruit clean and brush the surface with a layer of beaten egg white (don't over-beat this, though – it should be rich and smooth but not frothy). Then dust with caster (superfine) sugar, or a mixture of caster and granulated sugar, and leave the fruit to dry thoroughly to create the frosted effect. Large pieces will make a dramatic table display, but you can also frost grapes to hand round in little dishes as petits fours. Give redcurrants the same treatment to decorate a special dessert: they will glow like holly berries on the Christmas table but have the advantage of also being edible.

To complete the winter scene, combine the sparkling sugar frost with a dusting of soft, snowy icing. Traditional delicacies such as sugared jellies in pastel shades and rose-scented Turkish delight look irresistible if prettily displayed, and create a wonderful contrast to all the rich colours of the season.

Left: A plate of fruity sugared jellies, decorated by a simple gilded Christmas dove, provides a traditional treat to hand round at parties or at the end of a meal.

Right: A delectable arrangement of pears, plums, apples, figs and kumquats, frosted with sugar, is displayed in a glass pedestal dish for full effect.

Liquid gold

A glowing, aromatic punch is a must if you are to toast the season in style. Even the most abstemious revellers will find it hard to resist this traditional brew – as delicious in its colour and scent as in its warming, spicy flavour. It is the perfect drink to serve at parties, to revive chilled spirits after Boxing Day walks and to keep carol-singing excursions warm and merry. Best of all, the process of making it yourself, mixing your favourite combination of wines and liqueurs with fruit juices and spices, turns you into a modern-day alchemist, creating liquid gold out of everyday ingredients. It's all part of the magic of Christmas.

Each punch recipe has its special ingredients and you may have your own secret extras. The important thing is not simply to throw in all the leftover bottles from your drinks cabinet or last week's party and hope for the best. You need freshly opened wine, preferably a full-bodied red, but nothing too old or too oaky. If you haven't a favourite punch recipe of your own, try a basic combination of two bottles of red wine with 500ml (16fl oz, or 2 cups) of water, which will serve about 12 people. Add a clove-studded orange, the pared rind of half a lemon, 5ml (1 teaspoon) of powdered cinnamon, half a dozen lightly crushed cardamom pods, a quarter of a nutmeg (grated) and 100g (4oz, or ½ cup) of soft brown sugar. Simmer the punch for half an hour to let the spices infuse thoroughly, but don't let it boil or the alcohol will evaporate. Now add about 100ml (7 tablespoons) of brandy or an orange liqueur such as Cointreau, heat gently again and strain into a large, warmed bowl.

Left: Serve your hot punch in handled cups, which are easier to hold. If they are made of glass, make sure it is thick, and place a spoon in each one before pouring in the hot drink, to help prevent the glass from cracking.

Right: Have a warming bowl of mulled wine, flavoured with spices and a traditional clove-studded orange, ready to serve when the carol-singers call. Thin slices of orange floating on the top will make it look even more festive.

Oranges and lemons

Amid all the rich flavours of Christmas, the natural gold of bright, zesty oranges is
wonderfully refreshing. Stuffed into the toes of children's Christmas stockings or
served along with the chestnuts and chocolates, oranges (and their smaller cousins
satsumas, tangerines and clementines) are an intrinsic part of the celebrations. Use
their juicy flesh and aromatic peel to make additional treats and decorations, and
dry the cast-off peel to throw on the fire for extra scent. Squeeze them for
breakfast juice, eat them on their own or add them to fruit salads. Seville oranges,
with their more bitter taste, are perfect for marmalades and jellies.

For instant fragrance and a classic Christmas decoration, make traditional
pomanders that combine the sharp scent of the oranges with spicy cloves. Take an
orange (Sevilles are good for this, but you can vary the colour and scent by trying
kumquats and lemons, too) and use a knitting needle to prick rows of holes in the
peel. For the strongest scent, prick the entire orange, leaving about 6mm (¼in)
between each row. Or, for a lighter fragrance and to leave more colour showing,
prick in wider-spaced bands, marking the fruit into quarters or segments. Now
push a clove into each hole – right up to its head – and leave it to dry in a warm
place, such as in an airing cupboard or above a radiator, turning it occasionally to
maintain an even texture to the skin. Allow three or four weeks for it to dry
completely, then decorate with a ribbon.

Oranges can also be combined with nuts, cinnamon sticks and dried berries to
make garlands to hang on the tree or in a window. Score the oranges first, cutting
slits through the peel with a sharp knife so that the flesh is visible. Cut another
couple of oranges into slices. Then dry both scored oranges and slices – along with
a large handful of cranberries – by threading them onto thin skewers laid across a
roasting tin and baking them in a very cool oven until hard. Dry them in the same
way as the pomanders, then thread all the elements onto a length of garden twine
(drilling small holes through the nuts to take the twine, and tying bundles of
cinnamon sticks at intervals).

*Left: A spicy citrus garland in golden tones catches the winter light when hung in a window. Scored oranges and
lemons have been threaded together with nuts and spices and decorated with checked ribbon. To accentuate the
fragrance, paint the ingredients with aromatic oils.*

*Above right: Clove-studded oranges and lemons make old-fashioned pomanders to scent bedrooms and living
rooms. Decorated with pretty ribbon, they can be hung from a door handle, set on a tray or table, or wrapped in
cellophane and turned into tree presents.*

A touch of silver

Gilded fruits make a colourful addition to wreaths and swags as well as providing the perfect centrepiece for a festive table. Although not edible like the frosted fruits on page 74, these are every bit as glamorous, the metallic lustre transforming simple decorations into precious gems amid the greenery. Apples and pears work especially well, and bunches of grapes add a sense of real opulence. There are several ways of gilding them, but it is important to choose the firmest fruits you can find, especially with pears, which will soften rapidly once past their best.

The quickest technique is to rub a little gilt cream (available from craft and art shops) gently over the skin and foliage. If you wish, leave some of the green skin showing through, to give a more naturalistic effect. For a fully gilded look, spray the fruit or apply metal leaf.

Silver layered over gold creates a rich, antique finish. Spray the fruit with gold first, then paint it with a coat of size. When the size is tacky, apply sheets of silver leaf, brushing it onto the fruit in random patches so that the surface becomes a mixture of gold and silver.

Left: A selection of silvered fruits makes stunning decorations for the festive table. Arrange the fruits individually as a gift at each place setting, or pile them into a gleaming display in a fruit dish or on a stand. Combine with fresh or frosted fruits for an ultra-rich effect, and add sprays of greenery for contrast.

Right: Gilded and silvered fruits add an opulent touch to this wreath of garden greenery. The leaves have been frosted with white spray, then dusted with an extra coat of gold and silver, so that the fruits seem to grow naturally among them.

Glittering gifts

Gold is the most luxurious colour in which to wrap your presents. Rich and festive, it turns the simplest gift into something really tempting. Gold paper and gift boxes are the best place to start, but don't worry if you can't find them: plain brown parcel paper makes a surprisingly good substitute, and sheets of fine white tissue can be transformed with gold trimmings. Stick to this colour scheme and your presents will become decorations in their own right, gleaming like gold ingots when piled under the tree on Christmas morning.

Dressing up plain brown paper in a more glamorous role is one of the most satisfying ways to gift wrap. The paper has a slightly golden sheen to it anyway, because, if you look closely, there is usually a very fine stripe that acts as a highlight to the solid colour. It's easy to take this a step further by tying up the parcel in gold cord or ribbon, labelling it with a gold gift tag, and writing your message in gold ink. For extra glamour, attach a gold decoration too – a cluster of sprayed nuts or leaves, or even an ornament from the Christmas tree. Gold has natural associations with all sorts of seasonal images – stars, angels, bells and little harps or trumpets, for instance – and adding one of these to your wrapping will provide an additional gift for the recipient as well as making the package look more festive. Alternatively, if you prefer a more natural, country-style look to your presents, let the highlights of the paper make their own gold and then add simpler trimmings such as corn-coloured raffia ties and dried seedheads; wrapping like this is perfect for gardening gifts.

The paper itself can be decorated and patterned to create professional-looking designer effects if you feel plain white or brown is just too mundane for the occasion. Look for materials that make natural templates for the finish you want to create. Readymade stamps and stencils are available in a host of Christmas shapes, from fir trees and holly sprays to pine cones and mistletoe wreaths, but fallen leaves collected from the garden are just as useful. Working on a flat surface, lay them in position on the paper, then spray over them with gold so that the leaf outlines create a pattern. Paper doilies will add more intricate detailing, their cut-out decorations leaving a delicate snowflake effect on the plain background. These finishes work equally well on brown and white paper. Brown will look subtle and understated, but if you want the design to make more impact, go for a white background and a frosty, elegant look.

Right: Gold gift wrapping for a clutch of exciting presents, from plain brown paper with an overlay of sparkling cellophane to pure white tissue stencilled with gold stars. Trim your parcels with gold-sprayed berries and flower heads and tie them with luxurious braid or ribbon.

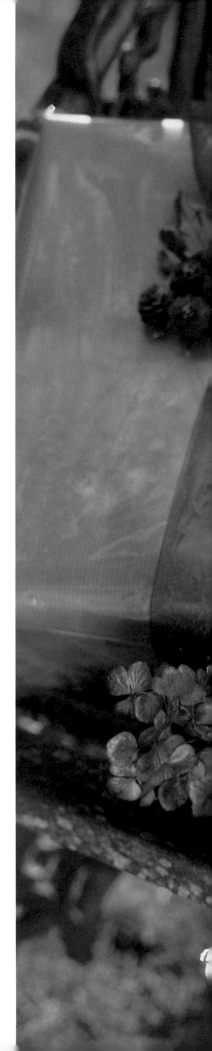

Comfort & Joy

Festive riches for traditional splendour

This is a look to fill your home with festivity. Bursting with colour and pattern, it's the traditional way to celebrate – a mixture of Victorian childhood memories of toy soldiers and Santas with the baroque splendour of opulent velvets, gold tassels and jewel-coloured decorations. Bold and joyful, it goes magnificently over the top, making the most of the opportunity to put on a show and indulge in a little luxury. The result is gloriously rich and welcoming. This is the nostalgic's Christmas, with old-fashioned angels and present-filled stockings hung on mantelpieces or brass bedsteads. It turns forgotten remnants like broken jewellery, old chandelier crystals, sewing box braids and scraps of velvet or brocade into sumptuous, glittering treasure trove.

Set the table with jewel-coloured glassware, add masses of candles for extra atmosphere and serve old-fashioned treats such as homemade jellies and hot chocolate. Rediscover your tartans and tapestries, silks and damasks, to provide the season's festive riches. Revive traditional rituals like designing your own cards, making candles and trimming the tree with handmade decorations.

As Christmas is about celebrating with family and friends, this chapter contains ideas for making sure guests feel comfortably at home. And because remembering the past year is as important as greeting the new one, there are suggestions for maintaining family traditions – including how to make a keepsake album that will let you record the details that have made Christmas so special.

Left: Gaudy gift wrapping in checks and tartans can be trimmed with opulent satin ribbons and colourful Victorian paper scraps, evoking childhood memories of a traditional Christmas.

Right: This buffet table set with sparkling coloured glass displays old-fashioned delights against a richly patterned background.

Handmade candles

Candles always add a sense of drama to the festivities. Their flickering flames bring the colours of your home to life, while their association with church contributes a joyful, celebratory significance. Scented candles, drenched with fragrance such as cinnamon and oranges, bring even more atmosphere. Group them together for the best effect, mixing different heights and sizes so that the flames create a haze of light in a corner, beside a fireplace, on your dining table or as part of a display of greenery and berries.

For extra richness, look out for handmade candles that incorporate seasonal colours and foliage. These will glow like stained glass as the wick burns down, letting the flame shine through the translucent wax and illuminate its contents. A similar effect can be created with candles made at home, allowing you to create a completely individual gift or table centrepiece.

You can make your own pillar candles using a basic glass, plastic or rubber mould and paraffin wax. It's easiest to buy or improvise moulds which either already have a hole in the base for the wick (the base becomes the top of the candle) or which can be pierced with a wicking needle to make the hole. Be sure to use the right thickness of wick for the diameter of the mould. The wicks need to be primed, so buy ready-primed wicks or prime them yourself by dipping them in melted wax. Thread the wick through the hole, using mould seal to secure the end on the underside and to seal the hole. With the wick taut, tie the other end to a pencil laid across the top of the mould. To help prevent dripping and make the candle easier to release from its mould, a little stearin is added (usually in the ratio of about one part stearin to ten parts wax). In a double boiler, melt the stearin, adding dye if required, then add the wax. Heat to a temperature of 82–93°C (180–200°F), then pour it into the mould. After a few minutes, tap the mould to release any air bubbles. The wax will set as it cools, but the process can be speeded up by standing the mould in a bowl of cool water. Break the skin that forms, and after an hour or so, use more melted wax to top up the well that has formed around the wick. When the wax has set completely, remove the mould seal; the candle should slide neatly out of the mould. Trim the wick to 6mm (¼in).

Basic pillar candles can now be decorated with beads, metal leaf or dried flowers. If you use flowers, attach the flower heads and leaves using tiny amounts of melted wax, making sure the petals lie completely flat against the candle. The candle will need an extra layer of wax to provide a protective finish for the flowers, so when your design is complete, dip it in melted wax and leave to cool.

Left: Bright red berries and silver-green fronds of yew and rosemary glow softly through the translucent wax of these decorative pillar candles. Grouped together on a mantelpiece, they reflect their flickering light back into the room and exude a delicious seasonal fragrance.

Glowing colour

Create a sense of traditional luxury both indoors and out by combining rich textures with glowing colours. Glossy berries contrast beautifully with velvety roses, and both have a festive opulence that is truly welcoming. The key is to use materials that are sympathetic to their surroundings, so that the elements reflect each other and work together to enrich the setting.

Look for blooms and berries in warm colours, and combine them with soft fabrics and textured backgrounds. Wreaths should be plump and full – for a gentle, old-fashioned effect, incorporate mixed flowers and foliage, or, for a circle of intense colour, simply mass berries together.

Trim your wreaths with ribbons in deep velvet or traditional tartan and introduce these fabrics in your furnishings, too, to complete the effect. Velvet or velour cushions and throws will look luxurious on chairs and window-sills. For richer pattern, mix in a few embroidered or tapestry cushions. These materials will look particularly wonderful against chestnut-coloured leather, so make the most of elderly furniture that has mellow, polished surfaces to offer – you are bound to need extra seating over the holiday period, so this is the time to remind yourself how comfortable those old leather chairs were.

If you have offcuts of flowers and foliage left over from your decorations, mix them into pot-pourri to set in pretty dishes around the house. Add pine cones and fir sprays from your Christmas tree, and sprinkle the mixture with oils that add festive scent, such as cinnamon and citrus.

Left: A luxurious wreath of deep red berries glows against the mellow gold of a faded stone wall. The crumbling surface makes the berries look even more sleek and glossy.

Right: A rambling old-fashioned wreath propped on a window-sill has berries and roses woven into it, some of them gathered into clusters, others held in little terracotta pots lined with moss.

Stained-glass effects

There is a sort of baroque splendour about traditional Christmas baubles. They are too glorious to restrict to the tree, so develop the concept further and find other ways to fill your home with jewel-like colours and iridescent surfaces. Glass balls can be displayed in dishes to look like fabulous glowing fruit (as long as you keep them out of children's reach) or used to add sparkle amid the greenery above pictures and doorways and in table arrangements. They are instantly nostalgic, too, conjuring up memories of Christmases long past. To reinforce this theme, fill little bowls with handfuls of old-fashioned marbles, mixing different sizes, colours and finishes – from the plain, transparent spheres with their twist of bright colour at the centre, to the marbles with reflective lustre finishes, sleek as ball-bearings. And don't forget those mysterious, misty designs that always seemed full of magic, like a witch's crystal ball.

Make the most of glass beads, too. Craft shops and catalogues sell a wonderful assortment of colours and shapes, from long spiky shards and tear-shaped droplets pierced with a single hanging hole to crystal-cut 'gems' designed for threading onto strings. Seek out your old jewellery: broken earrings, bracelets and necklaces relegated to the dressing-up box will provide a forgotten hoard of Christmas treasure just waiting to be rediscovered. Supplement them with newly bought additions if necessary and then use your finds to create your own unique decorations. Thread them together onto lengths of fine wire or metallic cord,

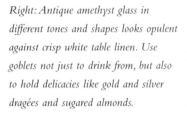

Right: Antique amethyst glass in different tones and shapes looks opulent against crisp white table linen. Use goblets not just to drink from, but also to hold delicacies like gold and silver dragées and sugared almonds.

Below left: A sparkling collection of beads and crystals for creating unique Christmas decorations.

mixing vibrant colours in different combinations just as you would if making them up into jewellery. Swag strings of beads around the tree so that it drips with coloured gemstones, weave them among the foliage when making front-door wreaths, suspend a garland below the mantelpiece or hang them in windows and from lamps so that they catch the light.

The effect you are creating is similar to the stained glass in a church window, and it's the way the colours react to the light that really brings them to life. Readymade accessories will all play their part too, so adapt your furnishings to complete the effect. Look for cut-crystal doorknobs, and curtain pole finials in coloured glass – amber, turquoise or amethyst – to replace even the most functional fittings with a sense of opulence. Buy sparkling beaded lampshades and candle holders to use on dinner tables and mantelpieces.

Below: A group of candles in coloured glass holders is offset by feathery fronds of cedar on this mantelpiece. The blue, red and yellow shades in the glass are highlighted by sparkling gold decoration.

Now for the dining table. Set it with coloured glassware, and you'll turn an everyday eating area into the setting for a feast. Dark plum and purple, rich cranberry and ruby, sparkling sapphire and emerald – all create a celebratory atmosphere which looks even more dramatic by candlelight. Nothing needs to be in matching sets: antique goblets and tumblers will mix very effectively with modern glassware, and the more variety there is, the richer the overall look. Silver and gold decoration provides sparkle, so look for glasses with gilded details, or serve tea and coffee in Viennese-style tumblers that have silver holders. Including a few lustre pieces will add a soft, iridescent gleam that reflects and diffuses the other colours. To illuminate it all for maximum impact, mass candles together on a mantelpiece or table where the multiple flames will intensify the coloured glow.

Below right: The rich wine colour of these glasses is made even more opulent by their flowing grapevine pattern and the glowing colour of the wall behind them.

'Twas the night before Christmas

Bedrooms are special places at Christmas. The main festivities may centre on the tree and the dining table, but it's in the bedrooms that stockings are hung up late on Christmas Eve, in delicious anticipation of the exciting shapes with which they will be bulging by the time morning comes. Never mind that the contents will have been leapt upon and their wrappings shredded well before breakfast (and possibly even before you are awake to share in the enjoyment) – that early-morning frenzy of present-opening is the first treat of the day and sets the tone for all the celebrations to follow.

Old-fashioned bedsteads are the perfect place to hang Christmas stockings – in fact, they could have been designed with that purpose in mind – but if you haven't any well-turned bedposts available, make the most of a mantelpiece instead. After all, this is where Santa will make his entrance so it is thoroughly appropriate (just remember not to light the fire).

Conventional stockings have never really provided enough room for the more awkward-shaped gifts, though, so many families resort to more generous-sized alternatives – from specially made stockings to pillowcases and sacks. Because no one ever properly grows out of the tradition of hanging up a stocking, don't leave adults out of the stocking ritual. Give them their own more sophisticated equivalent with drawstring velvet bags, or shawls and scarves tied into pouches. That way, you can make the stocking itself part of the present.

If you are having guests to stay during Christmas, their bedrooms will represent precious personal space in a houseful of people, so when you are preparing a spare room, try to think of it as a sitting room as well as a place to sleep. This will provide them with an oasis of calm amid the celebrations, and also help prevent them from feeling that they're constantly under their host's feet. Adding cushions and rugs – and an armchair if there's space – will instantly make guests feel more at home. Sprays of greenery above the bed and tucked behind pictures will keep up the Christmas spirit, while a well-chosen supply of books on a shelf or mantelpiece (rather than on the bedside table) will reassure them that they are welcome to sneak back here at any time if they feel in need of a little tranquillity during the course of the day.

Right: All the trappings of a traditional bedroom on Christmas Eve, with hand-stitched stockings cut from felt, and lengths of luxurious red and gold fabric creating improvised gift 'sacks'. A colourful patchwork quilt adds to the festive atmosphere.

Baubles and beads

Every family has its own traditions, and unpacking the tree decorations each year is a reminder of one of the most enjoyable – the intriguing assortment of baubles, stars, angels, toy soldiers and other ornaments that you have collected between you over Christmases past. As well as the sheer nostalgia of the memories they conjure up, there is a fascination about all the effort and intricacy that have gone into making them. Traditional glass balls – particularly the type with the silvered insets that sparkle like crystals – have never gone out of fashion, and the originals are now sought-after antiques. Little painted wooden toys add a Victorian childhood feel, and newer decorations – from electric candle lights to glitter-sprinkled snowflakes – add their own magic.

There will always be a special place for the homemade designs that remind us of particular Christmases and that year's craze – be it snowballs fluffed up out of white woolly pompoms, or cardboard angels with tinsel hair. It's never too late to revive the tradition and create new decorations. Craft catalogues sell polystyrene globes ready for you to transform with paint, glitter, beads and any other materials that will give your tree the flourish you want.

To create a traditional effect, reminiscent of the style in Victorian times, when the Christmas tree was first introduced to Britain, cover the polystyrene balls with layers of pasted tissue paper in different colours. For the richest effect, combine two toning colours on each one, so that the shade acquires more depth: mix cobalt blue and turquoise, emerald and amber, cerise and fuchsia. Wait until the paper is completely dry and the colours have gone back to their natural shade, then varnish each bauble to protect the design and give it a sleek, lacquered finish.

Now embellish each one with whatever finery you can find, such as gold braid and sparkling ribbon. Paste on Victorian scraps or motifs cut from wrapping paper. If you like, you can also add a discreet dusting of glitter at this stage, just on the area that you will designate as the top. Finally, thread two or three pearl or glass beads onto a hatpin and pierce the bauble (through the patch of glitter if you have made one) to create an ornamental top, then loop a wire around this to hang the bauble on the tree. Your brand-new ornaments will join the family's treasures, to be exclaimed over with pleasure as they are rediscovered each year.

Right: Paper roses, gilded angels and traditional Victorian scenes decorate these homemade tree baubles. Make a few extra, wrap them in tissue paper and package them in threes or fours as presents for friends.

Creative cards

Within the universal significance of the Christmas message, there are smaller, more personal joys to be celebrated. It's a time for remembering past years and special people, which is why the most symbolic way to mark it is with homemade gifts and cards. Think back to the days before mass-produced merchandise made Christmas shopping so convenient (and its results so anonymous) and take inspiration from the individually designed, painstakingly crafted novelties that were created each year in parlours and schoolrooms up and down the country.

Use the idea of the old-fashioned sampler to work a colourful card design in decorative stitches. The pattern is up to you: you could embroider Christmas images such as trees, holly sprays, jewelled crowns and bright robins, or stitch a festive message in traditional sampler-style lettering. Christmas sampler kits are available, containing linen or evenweave panels, coloured embroidery threads and printed designs for you to follow, but you can easily devise your own – all you need is a piece of plain fabric and a selection of threads. There is no need to hem the fabric edges: if you glue them onto a stiff paper or cardboard backing, they won't have a chance to fray. Better still, use a 'window' card that provides your sampler with a readymade frame. The lovely thing about an individual card like this is that it becomes a present as well: the recipient can frame it properly or put it away as a keepsake.

For a faster effect (and for those who don't feel so confident about their needlework), traditional Victorian scraps can still be bought in packs, and similar images can be photocopied in colour to cut out and stick onto stiff paper. Pressed flowers and leaves make beautiful decorations, too. Obviously the pressing process itself takes time, but if you have a supply of flowers already dried from the summer, this is a good way to use them.

Special-issue postage stamps always provide their own colour and decoration at Christmas, and you can use the designs to brighten up your cards as well as their envelopes. This needs some advance thinking, so start planning now for next year. Save the envelopes from the cards you receive and trim off the stamps (complete with their postmarks – the dates and locations add to the sense of occasion and the significance of the memory) to use in your own designs. An individual stamp on a coloured background will look simple and striking, or you can group them in a neat square or build up a collage effect of overlapping stamps.

To keep the whole occasion as special – and as personal – as possible, write your messages in pen and ink. Most of us resort to ballpoints and felt-tips for convenience, but it's fun to go back to the real thing once in a while. You could even use scented ink (from specialist stationery departments) for a festive flourish.

Right: The ritual of sending cards at Christmas is one of the last remnants of the letter-writing tradition, so enjoy it as an opportunity to exchange news with friends you have not seen during the past year.

Below: Create a completely unique Christmas card by embroidering the date and your family name on a square of cotton or linen. Frame the sampler with a needlework border of seasonal motifs and then set into a card mount.

A Christmas album

Commemorate the time you spend with family and friends by creating a
Christmas album to record the event. In future years you'll be able to look back
on a complete set of memories, bringing that Christmas to life almost as vividly
as if you could smell the mulled wine.

If you're a hoarder, it will come as second nature to you to hang on to any
particularly attractive cards you receive, gift tags accompanying presents you are
given, and thank-you notes for the gifts you sent. Collect all these together, and
add Christmas postage stamps, snippets of special wrapping paper and the ribbons
that trimmed them. Recipes can go into the album, too. Include old favourites
that you enjoy year after year, and also new discoveries that have proved a hit
and deserve to be repeated – this gives the collection a practical use as well as a
nostalgic value.

The very fact that you are capturing the spirit of the moment sets this
Christmas in the context of time moving on, so you don't need to make the
album look too much like an antique. As a modern twist to the Victorian tradition,
include informal snapshots taken during the celebrations, to remind you of the
occasion and the people you spent it with. Leave a few pages blank to record

*Left: Christmas cards have long been
collected and treasured. The first mass-
printed design was produced in the
mid-19th century, but even before
then, the Victorians enjoyed decorating
their visiting cards with brightly
printed paper scraps featuring robins
and holly.*

guests' messages, so that the album doubles as a visitors' book. Ask them to sign on their way out (it's a good idea to provide a good calligraphic or italic felt-tip pen, which will improve even the most spidery handwriting and make their comments worth preserving for posterity).

The album itself needs to be a good size and sturdy enough to stand the test of time. Look for books with good-quality paper, marbled endpapers, hand-cut edges and other luxurious features to make your collection feel extra-special. Or create your own loose-leaf book, which lets you add extra pages when you want to (this is a good idea if you prefer to keep one ongoing album rather than just commemorate a single year). Take a large pad of cartridge paper (poster board) and carefully hand-tear the paper into smaller pages. Cut two stiff covers from thick cardboard and decorate them with painted images or a découpage collage of Christmas scraps. When the paint or glue is dry, add a couple of coats of varnish, allowing it to dry between coats; this will protect the surface and make the album more robust. Finally, punch holes in both covers and in the pages, reinforcing them with metal eyelets. Thread a length of cord through the holes to bind the book, and finish with a couple of tassels.

Right: You can use an album to record your own memories of family Christmases or to start a collection of traditional festive memorabilia. Some antique cards are very delicate and will need to be carefully preserved, while others, such as early 20th-century Christmas and New Year postcards, are more robust.

Traditional treats

Delicious things to eat and drink are all part of the enjoyment of Christmas – making perfect presents as well as adding to the feast. Warming, spicy flavours will take the chill off crisp wintry days; tasty chutneys and preserves make the most of cold meats and hot toast; and chocolate, nuts and fruit are always irresistibly moreish throughout the holidays.

The most successful treats look as good as they taste, so aim for appetizing colours and pay attention to presentation – from the china or glassware you use to the garnish you add before serving. The simplest store-bought sweets (candy) can look stunning once their packaging is discarded and they are presented in a pretty dish. Homemade delicacies, of course, allow you to start from scratch in making them look as tempting as possible.

Preserves and pickles you have made yourself are among the nicest treats to prepare in time for Christmas, because of their traditional nature, long-lasting quality and attractive, old-fashioned appearance. Give a pot of glowing apple jelly or a flask of jewel-coloured fruit vinegar, and the gift will be enjoyed for months to come. Oranges, cranberries and raspberries will all infuse vinegar with their delicious flavours.

For orange vinegar, mix the juice and chopped peel of three large oranges in a saucepan with two 350ml (12fl oz, or 1½ cups) bottles of white wine vinegar. Bring it slowly to the boil, then cover and leave it in a cool place for two weeks. Strain the vinegar and decant it into elegant bottles, adding a spray of clean, dry fresh rosemary and a few peppercorns to each one before sealing.

For cranberry vinegar, pour a 350ml (12fl oz, or 1½ cups) bottle of white wine vinegar over 75g (3oz, or ½ cup) of dried cranberries in a mixing bowl, then cover the bowl and leave in a cool place for two weeks before straining and transferring to your presentation bottles. You can also add a few of the dried cranberries (or fresh cranberries cooked in a little of the vinegar and then left to cool).

Equally rich in colour, but designed to be served as a centrepiece rather than an accompaniment, are real fruit jellies, which looking stunning in elegant glasses. Make a syrup from 200g (7oz, or ⅞ cup) of sugar dissolved in 200ml (7fl oz, or ⅞ cup) boiling water. When it has cooled, add a 30g (1oz) sheet of gelatine, soaking it until soft then gently heating until fully dissolved. Stir in 900ml (30fl oz, or 3¾ cups) of freshly squeezed and strained orange juice mixed with 45ml (3 tablespoons) of squeezed and strained lemon juice – plus 30ml (2 tablespoons) of Grand Marnier or Cointreau if you want your jellies to have an extra kick – then strain again to make sure the liquid is clear. Pour it into glasses and chill for a few hours to set.

Jelly wedges are great fun for children. To make them, cut a few oranges in half from top to bottom, squeeze their juice and scoop out the flesh. Use the juice to make the jelly as above, adding a little extra gelatine for a firmer set. Pour the jelly

Left: Capture the festive flavour of oranges in traditional jellies. Whether served in glasses or cut into wedges, these make delicious party treats as well as providing a colourful finish to a celebration meal.

carefully into the orange 'cups' and chill until set. Slice into wedges with a very sharp knife just before serving. You can vary the colour of the jellies by using different types of orange, from the gold of navels and navelinas to the rich red of blood oranges.

Chocolate, too, has a magical quality. There's no other food that can be eaten on its own in chunks, grated over drinks and desserts, melted into both sweet and savoury dishes, or cooked as cakes, puddings and biscuits. There's bound to be a plentiful supply in your home at Christmas – some of it more delicious than the rest, but you can guarantee that even the cheapest, sickliest stuff will have disappeared by the end of the holiday.

Left: A warming cup of Viennese-style hot chocolate is especially delicious when topped with whipped cream and a generous sprinkling of grated bittersweet chocolate.

Right: A selection of colourful fruit vinegars labelled ready for Christmas. Collect suitable containers as you come across them, from cork-stoppered flasks to old-fashioned stone-topped bottles.

The finest bittersweet chocolate is a sophisticated indulgence and has the best flavour for treats such as Viennese-style hot chocolate. Prepare the whipped cream in advance by beating crème fraîche or double (heavy) cream with a little milk and caster (superfine) sugar until stiff; chill. Chop 160g (6oz) good-quality dark chocolate and melt over a low heat with a small pinch of salt and 60ml (2fl oz, or ¼ cup) water; don't let it burn. When smooth and shiny, stir in 500ml (16fl oz, or 2 cups) milk and 15ml (1 tablespoon) caster sugar. Bring to the boil and simmer for five minutes. Stir in 30ml (2 tablespoons) dark rum and 50ml (1¾fl oz, or a scant ¼ cup) espresso coffee. Boil for a few more minutes. Whisk the chocolate and pour into four cups. Top each cup with the cream, and grate chocolate over the top.

Here we come a-wassailing

Capture the sense of holiday and the spirit of childhood pleasures by dressing up in warm woollens and taking your celebrations out into the streets. The carol–singing tradition is one of the most enjoyable of the season: the combination of familiar music, good company and fresh air is wonderfully uplifting and can create a real sense of community. Even if you don't live in a village, you can capture that companionable spirit by establishing your own wassailing tradition with friends and family.

Proper carol singing (which means knowing the words and singing them with all your heart, rather than expecting to be rewarded for one verse of 'We Wish You a Merry Christmas') needs enthusiasm and organization. The carols, the route and the provisions all require planning. Choose a central repertoire of rousing carols that both singers and listeners know well, so that the singing is confident and the tunes instantly recognizable – the familiarity factor will trigger an instinctive sense of festivity. Then, if you're feeling adventurous (and have time to practise), you can add a few lesser-known songs. Traditional carols such as 'Masters in their Halls' and 'Here We Come A-Wassailing' are fun to try, and slower choruses – such as The Coventry Carol's 'Lullay, Lulla, Thou Little Tiny Child' – are sweet and melancholy if there's a good solo voice to sustain them.

Below left: Make sure young carollers are well wrapped up in warm hats, gloves and scarves.

Below and right: Dig out the lamps you usually reserve for power cuts and camping, and use them to illuminate the singers' route. Smaller lanterns can be fixed onto poles and held high to light the carol sheets.

Unless there are exceptionally good voices among you, aim for a large number of people to swell the song. Confident singing in a group where each voice is supported by the rest always sounds impressive. Even better, recruit a few musicians to join you, making the most of the available talent. If professional-standard violinists are thin on the ground, remember that flutes and recorders have a clear tone that makes up for any lack of expertise and adds to the general sense of merrymaking.

Candlelight makes the whole business much more atmospheric, so plan a route that's easy to negotiate after dark, and supply the choir with as many lanterns as possible. Oil lamps and traditional glass-sided candle lanterns are the most effective. Long candles can be hand-held if you create cardboard shields as protection from dripping wax. Cut a 15cm (6in) circle from stiff cardboard, make a small hole in the centre and then cut five or six short slits outwards from the hole so that you can fold the flaps back and push a candle through. The shield should grip the candle tightly and catch any dripping wax.

Keep the carollers fed and warmed with plenty of seasonal treats. Mince pies, little cooked sausages and roast chestnuts will turn the outing into a winter picnic, and mulled wine can be kept warm in vacuum flasks. For a children's and drivers' non-alcoholic punch, mix equal quantities of cranberry juice and lemonade, flavouring it with allspice, cinnamon and caster (superfine) sugar. If desired, a little grenadine can be added after the drink has simmered for about 15 minutes.

Themes & Ideas

Deck the halls with boughs of holly

★ *Left: Cut sprays of fresh bay leaves, trimming their stems to about 6mm (¼in) long, and weave them into a ready-made twig base, securing them with florist's wire if necessary.* ★ *Below left: Starting with a well-soaked moss base, build up an informal arrangement of ingredients such as pine sprays, eucalyptus leaves, chestnuts, walnuts, pine cones, cinnamon sticks and globe artichokes. Weave a wired ribbon through the finished wreath.* ★ *Below: Create a circle of wisteria cuttings and decorate it with rowan berries, moss, dried lavender, rosemary sprigs and hedgerow finds.*

★ *Right: Try a sparkling gold wreath against a plain cream background.*
A twist of gilded wire decorated with metal stars, suns and moons creates a
magical effect. ★ *Below: A simple twig garland painted white and woven*
with tumbling mistletoe is flanked by circles of evergreen box cuttings hung
on a Shaker-style peg-rail.

O Christmas tree, O Christmas tree!

★ *Below: Trim your tree with real candles for an old-fashioned celebration. Clip little tin holders onto the branches to highlight the glitter of the ornaments, making sure you position them so that the burning flames will not set light to the greenery.* ★ *Above right: For a cool, natural look, combine iridescent glass balls and garlands of white ribbon. The balls will act as rainbow bubbles, capturing miniature images of the room in their gleaming surfaces. Stand the tree in a decorative tin container to accent the silvery, reflective effect.* ★ *Below right: Turn a tiny Christmas tree into an instant present. Add whatever decorations you want, then plant it in a plain galvanized bucket and wrap in gold tissue paper.*

★ *Right: Give your tree a natural theme by combining dried-fruit decorations with fisherman's floats and a simple driftwood star. Hang the ornaments on ribbon and twine, and stand the tree in a country-style log basket.*

The holly bears a berry

★ *Left: Decorate holly berries and leaves with a dusting of gold and use the gilded sprays to trim your wrapped presents.* ★ *Near right: Highlight the glowing orange of physalis (Chinese lantern) berries by gilding the calyces that protect them. Gently pull the sepals apart and spread them out to create a starburst effect, then carefully add gold leaf or paint.* ★ *Below left: Tie your napkins with a length of bright ribbon and slip a sprig of guelder-rose berries under the bow or knot.* ★ *Below right: On a branch, hang a display of chandelier crystals and glass votive containers filled with berries of different colours.* ★ *Far right: Use lengths of variegated holly bearing plenty of berries for a colourful wreath to hang in a window.*

★ *Above: For the simplest homemade stocking, cut two shapes out of felt using pinking shears and top-stitch them together around the sides. Decorate the stocking with festive stars and Christmas trees in contrasting colours.* ★ *Left: Hang the children's stockings in a row across the fireplace, using leftover fabrics and trimming the tops with velvet ribbons and embroidered scraps.*

Bearing gifts we traverse afar

★ *Left: Stitch bright-coloured stockings from the children's favourite fabrics and add ribbons to tie them to the bedstead. (Don't forget to leave a glass of wine or a mince pie for Santa and a carrot for the reindeer.)* ★ *Right: Make use of old-fashioned blankets to create New England-style stockings, lining them with cheerful gingham.* ★ *Below: A stocking provides its own packaging, so presents don't all need to be wrapped. Allow a couple of toys to peep out of the top to make the stockings all the more exciting on Christmas morning.*

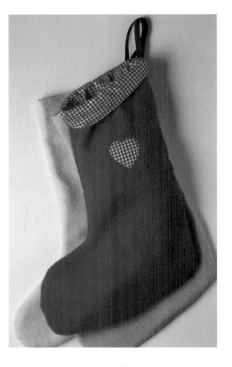

Star of wonder, star of night

★ *Above: Create a sparkling, frosty star to decorate a traditional ginger or chocolate cake by shaking a layer of sifted icing sugar through a stiff paper or cardboard template.* ★ *Below left: Use simple Shaker-style stars cut from painted wood or textured bark to give your tree a natural look.* ★ *Below centre: Make an elegant decoration by twisting a single length of wire into a series of concentric star shapes in decreasing sizes. Thread a glass bead onto the end of the wire for a glamorous finish and bend the tip over to hold the star in place.* ★ *Below right: Design your own gift tags or tree ornaments by tracing initials onto painted wood stars.*

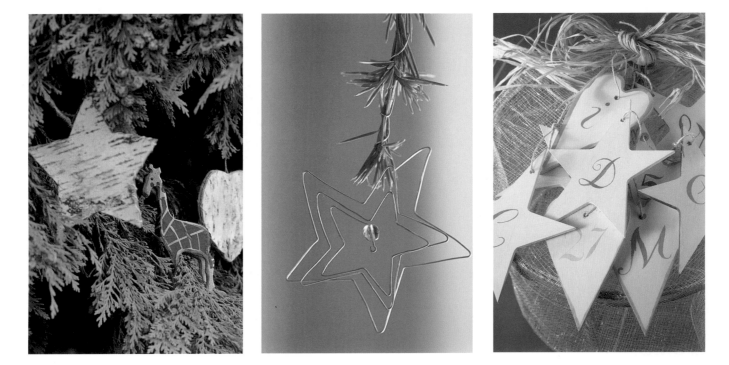

★ *Above: Create pressed-tin tree decorations by tracing a pattern into metal foil with a ballpoint pen.*
★ *Below left: Fold a rectangle of paper into narrow pleats, then fold the pleated paper in half and pin the centre with florist's wire. Cut across the two ends at an angle to form points, and fan the pleats out into a star.* ★ *Below right: Using pinking shears, cut star shapes from bright felt and stitch them together in pairs, lightly padded with cotton wool (absorbent cotton) or wadding (batting).*

★ *Above: For a special gift decoration, paint a wooden heart red, adding a coat of gold or yellow when dry, then scratching an angel design with a sharp knife. Sand lightly to remove the top colour partially and work it gently into the image, then wax to finish.* ★ *Left: Net-covered coat-hanger wings and a tinsel halo create the traditional trimmings of the Nativity play.*

Angels from the realms of glory

★ *Above left: Make your own tree fairy by dressing a rag doll with scraps of decorative lace. Make hair from embroidery thread and add a miniature twig wreath sprinkled with star-shaped sequins.* ★ *Above right: To make peg-doll angels, use old-fashioned clothes pegs (clothespins) as your base, making pipe-cleaner arms and adding tiny bundles of yarn for the hair. Cut wings from gold cardboard and dress your angels in lace or broderie anglaise (eyelet) trims.*
★ *Below left: For angel wings to fit a child, coat a sheet of fine tissue paper with wallpaper paste, then repeat with a second sheet on top. Arrange scraps of wrapping paper, lace, fabric, dried flowers, etc, on it, then cover with a third sheet; coat with paste. When dry, cut out (all in one piece) two wings with a 4cm (1½in) spine between them. Glue a cardboard cross with 2.5cm (1in) arms under the spine, trapping a long pair of ties at both top and bottom. Paint with clear oil-based varnish to stiffen.* ★ *Below right: For angelic place cards, cut out corrugated-cardboard wings, paint them with white emulsion (latex) and trace feathering into the finish before the paint is completely dry. Stick each wing onto a short piece of jeweller's wire, pierce the other two ends through a place card and twist back underneath to secure.*

Brightly shone the moon that night

★ *Above left: Design an elegant centrepiece by combining candles and greenery in a wire basket. Fill the basket with moss and add a crown of creamy roses to match the pale wax, then decorate with trailing ivy.* ★ *Above right: Surround a single pillar candle with an informal wreath of flowers and herbs. Soak and drain a floral-foam ring, add traditional evergreens to conceal it, then work roses, berries, crab apples and aromatic herbs into the arrangement.* ★ *Below left: Trim a little wire tree with votives held in sparkling glass holders.* ★ *Below right: Display handfuls of slim tapers in decorative glasses. A little water in the glasses will hold them steady; stand the glasses in a shallow silvered tray to reflect the flickering light and catch dripping wax.*

★ *Right: Mass plain white candles together in crystal and cut-glass holders so that they catch the light of each other's flames for a glittering, sparkling appearance. There's no need for them to match – use as many different heights as possible, as though filling the canvas of a picture. If possible, stand them in front of a large mirror to multiply the effect.* ★ *Below: Accent interesting architectural features with the subtle glow of candlelight. Stand chunky pillar candles in a carved niche to illuminate the colour and texture of the surrounding wall. Nestle them among cushions of moss and fronds of dark evergreen for a natural, woodland setting.*

index

Page numbers in *italics* refer to photographs.

Photographic Acknowledgments

Caroline Arber: pages 1, 13, 18, 25, 27, 41, 52, 54 (left), 56 (left and right), 63, 83, 91, 95, 110, 115 (right), 116 (bottom left), 119 (top left), 120 (bottom centre), 121 (bottom left and right), 123 (top right and bottom right), 124 (top left)

Tony Boase: page 44

Jon Bouchier: pages 117, 118 (right)

Charlie Colmer: pages 15, 20, 21, 26, 35 (left), 43, 47, 50, 58, 59, 68, 69, 70, 72, 74, 79, 87, 97, 115 (bottom left), 125 (right)

Harry Cory-Wright: pages 10, 22 (right), 78, 93, 112 (bottom left and bottom right)

Steve Dalton: page 101

Melanie Eclare: page 8

Polly Eltes: page 37

Laurie Evans: pages 32, 76, 77, 106

Craig Fordham: pages 19 (left and right), 108 (left and right), 109

Kate Gadsby: pages 46, 116 (bottom right)

David George: pages 23, 30, 84, 85, 94, 114, 118 (left), 119 (bottom), 124 (bottom right)

Jacqui Hurst: pages 111, 116 (top left and right), 121 (top)

Sandra Lousada: page 122 (left)

James Merrell: pages 22 (left), 40, 41, 64, 65, 86, 92, 113 (top and bottom), 115 (top left)

Debbie Patterson: pages 24, 112 (top), 120 (bottom left)

Bridget Peirson: page 48

Trevor Richards: pages 107, 120 (bottom right)

Kim Sayer: pages 62, 71, 80, 81

Debi Treloar: pages 11, 31, 88, 102, 122 (right), 123 (top left and bottom left)

Pia Tryde: pages 3, 5, 7, 12, 14, 16, 17, 28, 29, 38, 39, 51, 53, 54 (right), 55, 61, 66, 75, 90, 99, 103, 124 (bottom left), 125 (left)

Peter Williams: pages 33, 34, 35 (right), 60, 104, 120 (top)

Ling Wong: pages 36 (left and right), 119 (top right)

Polly Wreford: page 100

Styling by Pippa Rimmer, Hester Page, Ben Kendrick, Kate Charlwood, Caroline Zoob, Carl Braganza, Kristin Peres, Julia Bird, Jayne Keeley, Jemima Mills, Nicola Goodwin, Gabi Tubbs, Eliza Wheatley, Jane Packer and Carol Peters.